A Far Off Bell

GLADYS O'CONNOR

Copyright © 2018

Originally published 1987 by HUTTON PRESS Ltd.

This edition designed and edited by Philip Atkinson.

All rights reserved.

A FAR OFF BELL

by Gladys O'Connor

This edition © Copyright 2018

No part of this book may be reproduced, stored in a retrieval system or transmitted in any form, all by any means electronic, mechanical, photocopying, recording or otherwise without the prior permission of the publisher and the copyright holder.

PREFACE

A few years ago, by the kind courtesy of the headmaster, I was invited to look around his new comprehensive school. It was really splendid—light, well-equipped and tastefully furnished. Its pupils looked alert, happy and neat in their uniforms.

The school was of special interest to me as it is built on the exact side of what was my childhood home more than seventy years ago. But that home, an ancient farmhouse (it was reputed that some of Cromwell's supporters had stayed there)—had been surrounded by fertile farmland, not another house within a mile, while the school is within the bounds of a firmly established New Town, population over 20,000, with large industrial areas, shopping precincts, parks, churches and 'all mod cons.'

After this visit I kept on recording the old days and marvelling at all the changes brought about after two world wars and seventy-odd years. There was nothing for it but to try to record them.

Though basically factual, fiction and childhood memories and interpretations have become interwoven with fact. The characters described are fictitious but resemble in many ways the remembered people of that day and their way of life.

A mile from Lowridge, a small village in the north of England, was the ancient farmhouse of Greenfield, pleasantly situated amongst ancient brooks, beeches and elms and almost two-hundred acres of good land calling out for good husbandry, which had been lacking for several years. So, at the beginning of the twentieth century Thomas Crosby, his wife Rachel and their nine children became the tenants, an undertaking which was to take many years of toil and sweat —and no little pride—to restore it to a very commendable standard.

The family became well-known and respected in the district. Thomas, a rather stern and reserved man, was, however, public-spirited and took an active concern in matters of interest in the village and among the neighbouring farmers. Being up to date in farming methods, his advice was often sought, and he helped to solve veterinary or very simple legal matters on request. He caused quite a stir of excitement when he bought the first self-binder harvest machine to be seen in that district, and many came to marvel at its wonders.

Rachel, cheery and hard-working mother of their large and lively brood, had little time or inclination for outside interests beyond her church-going, and infrequent visits to the small market town Oakdale. But she was well liked by all who knew her, and particularly by the needy families of the hamlet of Rockyburn, who often benefited from her generosity both of sensible advice and practical help. Her happiest times were when her family were around her, and when her sisters came to stay, bringing glimpses of their lifestyle but in no way causing her to envy them. She had a contented nature deriving strength and comfort from her firm Christian faith and beliefs. She was also blessed with a ready sense of humour which her family appreciated and shared.

The nine children had derived all the benefit possible from their elementary school education, extended by wide-reading and 'night school.' Some proceeded to grammar school if only for the limited time the farm could spare them. Though of necessity 'home-keeping youths' they did not suffer from 'home-keeping wits.'

When Anna's story begins, the oldest son, Edward, now married, had opted out of farming to become a butcher; John had been to college and was teaching in a distant town. As boys, both had done their share of hard work on the farm, but it could not support them to the extent of paying them wages, nor did it interest them. The girls stayed at home till they married, also working for no more than pocket-money.

After a longer interval than usual between the family's birthdays, Anna was born, to be dubbed the Post Script, and was eight years old in 1913 when her story begins.

G. O'Connor
May 1987

CHAPTER ONE

HOLIDAYS OVER

Anna felt that gentle push in the middle of her back and awoke at once, sleep banished instantly, for after eleven hours of it who needs more? The push came from her grown-up sister, Zilla, with whom she shared the black iron brass-knobbed double bed.

"Time to get up—school again," said Zilla, who, because of poor health, was allowed to lie longer.

"I know," Anna replied cheerfully as she slid from under the bed clothes, her feet briefly enjoying the soft curly lambskin rug at the bedside. She stepped onto the cool, well worn, once gaudily-coloured oilcloth and went to gaze out of the open window. The lace curtains were gently moving in and out like someone breathing, for the August morning was almost without breeze and already at half-past seven a hot day was betokened. A delightful miscellany of country scents was wafted in with the motion of the curtains, scents of phlox, roses, new haystacks and dewy grass. Anna drew a great deep breath of pure pleasure.

She slipped out of her flowered cotton nightdress, into her cotton, home-made underclothes, and then excitedly into a new school dress. She turned to the small mirror on the dressing table, swinging it this way and that to view herself from different angles. Delighted with the results she returned to the bedside to show it off to Zilla, who in her soft, gentle voice said, "It's nice; you look bonny in it."

The dress was of a dark blue serge-like material, long sleeved and with scarlet collar, cuffs and patch pockets. A shiny red leather belt completed the picture.

"Our Mary's clever, isn't she?" said Anna admiringly, and Zilla smiled agreement.

Mary and Dot, who had much earlier vacated the other double bed diagonally opposite theirs, were two more of Anna's big sisters, Dot being sixteen and Mary twenty-one.

Mary had made the dress as indeed she had made all Anna's clothes for as long as she could remember.

A voice from downstairs urged Anna to hurry up, so hastily dabbling hands and face in the cold water which she poured into one big china bowl from a matching jug on the washstand and sketchily drying, she raced down.

Already most of the family had breakfasted in the big farmhouse kitchen and gone out to work. Anna's plump, rosy-faced mother and Dot were still seated at the long table which was covered with brightly coloured, shiny oilcloth and the debris of the previous sitting.

The new dress was duly admired, a pinafore donned to protect it, Anna's long fair hair plaited into neat plaits and tied with new red ribbons. She put on well polished black-buttoned shoes, pulling her knitted grey woollen stockings up to her knees. Then she sat down to a breakfast of fried egg, bread and a cup of milk.

"Well, Anna," said her mother, "School again. You had a grand long holiday so now you must work hard."

Anna finished crunching a mouthful of the tasty fried bread and said in a somewhat prim little voice, "I always do."

"Huh," was Dot's only comment.

Just then Hugh, their fifteen-year-old brother, appeared in the doorway, bound for the dairy with two pails of warm frothy milk.

"Hello shrimp," he greeted Anna. "Going somewhere?"

Anna pointedly ignored him. Although she adored him she didn't always feel she needed show it. Hugh went to grammar school and still had some holiday left, which was a rather sore point with his young sister.

"Up the garden," commanded Dot as Anna drained the cup of milk, and Anna obediently went to perform her natural duties at the 'closet', which was tiny house embowered with ivy and rambler roses.

At last, with a few pieces of advice about working hard, keeping her new dress nice, hurrying home after school, and some messages for her married eldest sister at whose home in the village she would have her midday meal—to all of which

Anna only half listened—she was off, eager and happy to start a new year at the village school.

As she passed through the farmyard, Steve, her red headed, suntanned brother, gave her a shout and wave. Steve was really her favourite of all the family, she thought, or anyway perhaps just the tiniest bit more adored than Hughie. He was twenty, and so strong and nice-looking, and he had such a lovely voice and he read the lessons at church better even than the parson or the schoolmaster. All the village girls were mad about him, but *she* knew whom he liked best! Anna's thoughts ran on happily as she crossed the pasture, over a shallow stream, along the path at the edge of a corn field where the stooks of ripened wheat stood like little tents. Another field and then a short narrow lane shaded by ash, beech and sycamore so that it was like a cool green tunnel.

This lane led into a wider main road, though its potholes, bumps and cracks showed little maintenance. The road connected the small hamlet of Rockyburn to the village of Lowridge where the school was.

Little gangs of poorly-clad children were making their way along the road, but on this morning Anna took little notice of them or they of her. She was eager to join her best friend, Elsie, who no doubt would be setting off from the village to meet her. They had spent a great part of the holiday in each other's company, but nevertheless they would have lots to talk about, for at eight years of age life is 'so full of a number of things' that need to be discussed. Besides, Elsie and Anna each had a wonderful new dress that they were dying to show off. Sure enough, there was Elsie coming round the bend in the road. The two friends ran gleefully to meet, coming to a laughing halt face-to-face and avidly taking in each other's appearance.

"Ohh! Yours is nice, Elsie!"

"So is yours—smart! Turn around!"

They pointed out all the attractions of their dresses. Elsie's was of a black and white checked material with pleats and a white lace collar which, she explained, was detachable, and she had two more to change with it. Anna was too kind to ask if the dress was new, because she guessed it was a gift from Elsie's 'rich friends' and no doubt before the day was out Elsie would have confided this to her. So, highly satisfied, each with her own and the other's stylish outfit, and ready to display their splendours to less fortunate acquaintances, they turned their attention schoolwards.

The bell was now ringing, calling the stragglers along the road, the village children and several from distant farms to hasten to partake of the fare, educational and ecclesiastical, offered by Lowridge Church of England school in the year 1913.

Anna and Elsie joined hands, swinging them and skipping to the rhythm of the words they chanted:

"Tin! Tin! Tin!
I'm made of
Tin! Tin! Tin!
Mind if you're late
You'll get the
Cane! Cane! Cane!"

They had made up this rhyme and thought it very witty and apt. They were wrong in their first statement however, for the bell was made of good true metal benefiting a bell that served on Sundays to call the same communities to worship, for on Sunday school became church as the parish church was a good two miles away at Thickley. As for their second statement that was only too true.

CHAPTER TWO

LOWRIDGE

The school stood at the end of Lowridge (by any standards a poor and unattractive place) at right angles to the two long rows of shabby, nondescript cottages bordering a wide green, through the middle of which ran a potholed road. The rows, named unimaginatively Northside and Southside, opened straight onto a rough pavement at the edge of the green and displayed no pretty cottage gardens to the passerby, although many of them had a pretty enough patch at the back.

There were also two short side-streets, a grim-looking Methodist chapel, a derelict small coal mine and its accompanying slag heap and partly dismantled machinery. The only building with a really pleasing appearance was a large, creeper-covered house in a walled garden and the square stone farmhouse set well back from the green and approached by a drive edged with rhododendrons and other flowering shrubs. Two public houses, a butcher shop, two small general dealer shops and another farm house made up the village.

The schoolmaster's house was just one of the Northside row, little bigger than the rest and distinguished mainly by its one bay window, and, this August morning, by its newly acquired, startling yellow, grained paintwork.

The villagers were poor too. They were mostly farmworkers on near starvation wages, or railwaymen at the large sidings at Thickley, with little better pay but no perks such as a few eggs and the odd pint of milk. Many others were simply odd job men who had never had regular work since the pit had closed. These, and their families, existed on the most meagre scale, picking up a shilling or two here and there on the farms at hay or corn harvest, potato picking or corn threshing. The most poverty-stricken would be 'on the parish' which was just one step above starvation. Some of the villagers kept a few hens, and even a pig to add a welcome luxury to their larders when, by miraculous management, their owners had fattened them up to a reasonable size for slaughter.

Rabbits and hares, pheasants and partridges were plentiful in the surrounding fields and woods and poaching was the order of the day—or night—until a policeman came to live in the village to cooperate with the gamekeepers of the local 'gentry'. But even his advent could not, and did not, foil the exploits of hungry men, and whilst he was stalking the poachers it was an opportunity for others to help themselves to some farmer's potatoes or turnips, useful ingredients for the stew pot even without meat!

Back gardens produced other vegetables, and some boasted an apple, pear or plum tree, raspberries and currants, so by and large they did not starve, though as one wit said they would mostly be 'streaky bacon' like their pigs, which had good days and bad where food was concerned.

Lowridge was poor in that it lacked that pleasant future of most English villages—water. There was neither a pebbly babbling brook nor even the placid waters of a common duckpond. Trees too were missing, but pleasant tree-lined lanes with high hedges led to the hamlet and farms outside.

But in spite of its lack of many amenities and anything approaching wealth, it was, in the main, a neighbourly village. Most of the families had lived there for several generations and there had been much inter-marrying. No one had to ask twice for help in times of trouble, sickness or loss. Family rows and feuds, where they occurred, were often healed by the sharing of a common catastrophe or accident. A 'fisty-fight' would be forgotten over a pint at one of the village's pubs. A happy event, like a wedding, a new baby, or recovery from illness, was enjoyed by all, and small gifts were produced from the most meagre of budgets. Chapel folk and Church people were not conspicuously united, though neither were they noticeably divided, except perhaps when either arranged a field day or a seaside outing, and then there was muttering and debating whether 'so-and-so's bairn should be going being 'neither one nor t'other,' but generosity sometimes won. Harvest festival at either church could expect an unusually large mixed congregation.

Anna's farm, Greenfield, a mile distant, was in her opinion the loveliest farm in the world. It was an ancient house, many-angled and spreading, of warm-tinted stone and nestled among beautiful beeches, elms, ash and oaks. More than one stream wandered through its fields, and ponds hedged with wild roses, honeysuckle and wild iris provided frogspawn and water boatmen, and on summer nights a chorus from the happy frogs.

It was said that Cromwell's men had stayed in the house and that some of his 'high-up' leaders had occupied a more elegant mansion a few miles away. Be that as it may, Anna thought it quite perfect—together with her family, of course!

Her parents, by no means well off having brought up so large a family, were highly respected in the neighbourhood. Anna's father's advice was sought on many matters, particularly concerned with farming, veterinary problems and small legal points. He caused quite a stir of excitement when he bought the first self-binder harvest machine to be seen in that part of the county, and many came to marvel at its wonders.

Besides this, both her father and mother believed in *education* and they read *books*! An older brother had been to college and was now a teacher in a town some miles distant. Steve had gone to grammar school until he was sixteen when the farm had claimed him. Dot had passed the scholarship but had only been able to go to high school until she was fourteen, the farm having needed her unpaid help too. The farm was now paying a little better so that Father said that even if Anna didn't get a scholarship he could pay for her to go to the high school.

There wasn't another such home or family in Lowridge, or anywhere else for that matter, thought Anna. And another thing—they had a piano and she was having music lessons!

Elsie's home in the village was one of the small cottages of Northside. Her father, being a draughtsman at the railway works was better off than many of their neighbours and their house was always well painted, neat and comfortably furnished. They too had piano, which Elsie's father played very well. Elsie was having lessons and hinted that she might have singing lessons some day. She too was proud of her parents—her father because of his superior job and his musical talent, and her mother because she knew all about *manners*!

Before her marriage Elsie's mother had been a lady's maid at Winstone Hall, the home of local titled people, where she had to learn manners and ideas far removed from those of her village neighbours. These 'ladylike' manners she had passed on to Elsie, their only child, so that should occasion for putting them into practice ever arise Elsie would rise to it and do them all credit.

These favourable conditions shared by the two friends made them feel a bit different from most of their schoolmates—a kind of innocent superiority which was neither snobbishness nor conceit but rather a happy awareness of their good luck. It did not in any way detract from their popularity for both had many friends in the school where the new scholastic year was now about to begin.

CHAPTER THREE

THE SCHOOL

As the last 'tins' of the bell died away, some one-hundred-and-twenty children had gathered in front of the school, a grim and plain red brick building. On this day the children, mostly poorly clad, and some in little better than rags, and aged from five to fourteen years, were standing aimlessly around, or pushing and chattering, making a half-hearted attempt at getting into 'lines.' A few very small new starters were looking very apprehensively at the big ones.

A young woman appeared in the doorway, blew a piercing blast on a whistle and yelled, "Lines!"

The talking stopped and the children arranged themselves into five passably straight lines, Infants at the front.

"Turn!" shouted Miss Manley

Big and little boots and a few bare feet shuffled in a right turn.

"March!"

In trotted the little ones encouraged by some un-gentle shoves from the children behind. Soon, all except the Infants, who had their own room, were assembled in the 'big room' for the opening session.

This long room was in fact made up of two divided by a sliding screen, the top half glass and the lower of yellowish green wood which had obviously shared the same decorator as the schoolmaster's house.

One room was very small and was elevated by two steps. Above the screen framing this room was a flowery, ornate inscription, 'My House is the House of Prayer,' for on Sundays this small room was the chancel and choir stalls. It contained a number of furnishings for church in a big locked cupboard, a pulpit-cum-lectern, and a small organ, also locked during the week, in a case with the same curly-cues as the inscription above the screen. Seldom used as a classroom it was something of a mystery to those children who had never been to a church service and seen it in its Sunday glory. They call it 'The 'oly Room'.

High windows, arched like the front door, let in light, were seldom opened to admit air and afforded no view of the outside except the sky to any but the tallest pupils.

Now Mr. Black the schoolmaster appeared, flanked on one side by Miss Stewart, teacher of Standards 3 and 4, and on the other by a pretty, 17-year-old village girl who had been to the high school and was now to begin a year as pupil teacher before going to training college. Her name was Betty Butterfield, and Standards 1 and 2 were to be entrusted to her. The master himself was responsible for Standards 5, 6 and 7.

Mr. Black was a smallish, sturdily built man in his early forties. If his usual expression had not been so dour he would have passed as handsome, but, the children said, he was 'Black by name and black by nature,' no doubt quoting their parents. His hair was jet black, his skin rather sallow and often dark with a quick-growing shadow of stubble, and alas often darkened with rage, for he was subject to outbursts of violent temper which brought the blood to his face in an alarming manner. Apparently in perpetual mourning he wore a black tie with his sombre navy-blue serge suit into the waistcoat armhole of which was hooked the fearful cane of Anna and Elsie's rhyme.

After 'Good morning's' had been exchanged with a cheerfulness that would seldom be so manifest in the rest of the term, Betty Butterfield seated herself at the piano, and the children sang happily:

"For-thin Thy Name O-Lor-die-go," being stopped in the second verse while the Master bawled at a child for not singing. Then on again, lustily, to the end. A collect was said by the Master, followed by the school's repetition of the Lord's Prayer, again interrupted—"How many times have I to tell you it's not 'tem-er-tation?' Start again!"

A short address followed, mainly to exhort the boys and girls to be regular in their attendance and to do their best. Then "Classes!" barked Mr. Black, whereupon Betty

Butterfield began to lead out her little ones to a room built out at the back, Miss Stewart's flock making for another side room. The rest waited while half-a-dozen big boys rattled the screens into place.

But stop! Who is this daring to enter? Daring is scarcely the right word—dreading is nearer the mark. Two little late-comers, two dirty, ragged little lads from the slum-like Rockyburn wriggle through the hardly-open door and stand rooted to the spot in terror.

"Come here!" commands Mr. Black in a voice that chills, whilst slapping his leg ominously with his cane. The miscreants creep towards him, practically hypnotised. The rest of the children are still, some holding their breath tensely, others impatient and even indifferent, an attitude born of familiarity with such scenes.

"Well. Where have you been?" Pause. "Speak up!"

A moistening of dry lips, and a frightened squeak.

"Please sir, our mam's bad and she couldn't get up."

"But YOU could, couldn't you?"

No answer.

"Speak up!"—in a voice of thunder.

Still no answer.

"Hold out your hands then, if you can't speak. Both hands —one for being late and one for not answering me."

Four dirty little palms were held out tremblingly, and swish! down came the vicious cane—one, two, three, four; in truth not with great force but the fear already induced made it seem so.

The two small boys, hugging their stinging hands under their armpits, and weeping loudly, went to join their new and soft-hearted young teacher. Once safely in her room she wiped their tear stained little faces thereby making them considerably cleaner, and promised them a sweet at playtime.

"I hate him," Anna, trembling but vehement, whispered to Elsie.

"Me too, big old pig!" replied her friend, with a grimace that was anything but ladylike.

"You shouldn't," came back a jeering whisper from Jim Tracer. "Teacher's pets, both of you!"

"Grrr!" All the scorn in the world was in Elsie's comment on this. But there was a grain of truth in Jim's remark as both girls knew well. Although it was a fact, which he would certainly have denied having been put to him, Robert Black always favoured clean, pretty little girls from 'better' homes. There were a few of these, indeed a score at most, so they were easily identified by the less favoured though with little rancour or envy, for to be *his* pets held little attraction for any of them. In their simple wisdom they preferred to be quite independent of the tyrant.

Favourites or not, however, he never caned a girl, clean, pretty or otherwise.

On this first day of new school, Anna and Elsie were to be in Standard 4 with Miss Stewart. Hers was a small room with rows of dual desks and little of interest. Even the window sills were too narrow to accommodate all but the smallest of jam jars, now empty but soon to display flowers, twigs and bulbs and any other object of natural history available locally.

There were a few non-descript pictures. One of these was of the late King Edward and Queen Alexandra; another of Lady V (Elsie's mother's pinup), who was one of the school's governors. Only two had any pretensions to attractiveness or interest for the children. One was a pretty country scene with a flower-fringed brook. This Anna began to identify with Tennyson's 'Brook', from the poem which she soon knew by heart. The second, which she found entrancing, was a dreamlike fantasy called 'The Plains of Heaven.' Soon, however, some of the pupils' artistic efforts would be pinned up on the pitch-pine surround. Blackboard easel, the teacher's desk, a large cupboard and accounting frame completed the furnishings. Hot water pipes heated the room for the winter months.

The two friends having 'come top' in their previous class were allowed to choose their seats. Indeed they had always shared a dual desk and many whispered secrets. Naturally they picked the desk furthest away from Miss Stewart's so that their whisperings and giggles would more easily escape that lady's keen ears and eyes. Over the gangway next to them sat their two boy-friends, Willie and Harry, likewise privileged to choose their seat. Another twenty or so boys and girls filled the remaining seats, or should have done had there not been so many habitual absentees.

CHAPTER FOUR

THE CURRICULUM

The first lesson on the timetable never varied, term in term out. It was 'Scripture" and involved a deep, thorough and uncompromising grounding in Bible stories and in Church doctrines as set out in the Book of Common Prayer—in particular the Catechism, which had to be memorised in sections throughout the different classes. Bible stories from Old and New Testaments were to be memorised and retold almost verbatim. Innumerable Bible passages, psalms and hymns proper to the Church's year were learnt.

As it was not considered necessary to provide very explicit meanings of these hymns many of the words were little better than a foreign language to the less bright children. Anna, a regular churchgoer, often read through the hymns to while away the time in tedious sermons. She had many a stifled chuckle when she realised how the children's versions differed from the printed word.

'Half the whole good angels sing…'

'The angel host pork then…'

'Pardon all our faces…'

'By our boat call slowly…'

Once a week the vicar or one of his curates from Thickley would come to take 'scripture,' hear a hymn or two and a part of the Catechism. They would tell the children to obey their parents and teachers and to come to church regularly. "Yes, Sir!" The children chorus obligingly but without the least intention of carrying out any of their injunctions.

'Songs' followed. For several minutes a pleasant sing-song issued from each room as the various classes 'did' their tables, ranging from 'twice times' through pounds-shillings-and-pence, 'averderpoys,' long measure and 'C-pasty.'

Anna and Elsie liked arithmetic and rattled away with pounds shillings and pence *and* farthings with nonchalant ease, filling both sides of their slates, having them marked almost always correct—a wipe with the soggy sponge and away to fill the slate again.

If there was a difficulty Anna could always count on the help of her nicest boy-friend, Willie Smart, for he was smart at sums and most other subjects too. Leaning across the gangway he was quick to detect a mistake on her slate. A tug at her fair plaits, a whispered hint and—Woosh!—rub it off and start again. This wasn't easy in Miss Stewart's class—they had already had a year with her and knew her ways. They knew she had her work cut out with two classes and that she was only too pleased that Willie could save her precious time. He could even be relied on to teach the girls the next step as he was always one or two jumps ahead.

Roars and crashes were heard from next door where Mr. Black was instructing the top classes alternately in long multiplication, division, fractions, decimals and even simple interest to the most able. He drove home his points by yells and slamming the blackboard with his cane. Strangely enough his crude methods brought forth some fruit and a few of the brightest children became very proficient at mechanical processes and really enjoyed 'sums.' But woe-betide the dull ones, whose name was legion; arithmetic was pain and grief to them and many a slate was washed with tears. Slates were used by all but the best pupils who were privileged to use squared exercise books. There was, however, a set of exercise books that was used every 'Black Friday' for a test. These had to be treated with the greatest care that they might be presented without spot or blemish to His Majesty's inspectors whenever the school might have the misfortune to receive one of their unannounced visitations.

And so the lessons moved heavily on to ever welcome playtime, when pent up energy, griefs and fears could be worked off in rough, noisy games, fights and horseplay.

Anna and Elsie sometimes joined in the noisy fun, enjoying the wild chasing and knock-about games with the boys, but more often were teamed up with Jennie who lived at the farm adjoining Greenfield, and with some of the village girls for skipping, hitchy-bay, singing games and buttony. The latter, as its name implied, required a number of buttons and often involved taking the odd one off someone's coat in the porch when hard pressed. However most of the coats were so shabby that a snatched button or two were never missed.

On the lucky occasions when one of the girls had a penny or ha'penny to spend they would risk a quick dash to the village shop. This was definitely out of bounds but could be reached with speed and cunning. A penny could buy long strands of liquorice 'bootlaces' which were snapped into short lengths and shared amongst best friends; a bar of delicious cream chocolate cost a penny but did not share out so well. Then there were novelties like 'dinners,' which consisted of a cardboard plate on which were stuck miniature but realistic looking potatoes, peas, carrots and a chop, made of a rather tasteless sweet paste. This cost all of two pence. A large striped minty humbug was another choice but rather difficult to conceal from the teacher or to share. Aniseed balls were interesting, revealing different colours as they were sucked smaller and smaller, eventually ending in white ball the size of a pinhead.

What sticky pockets resulted from these excursions! What a dash to get back to the playground in time for lines! If the sweets where not always worth the money the excitement certainly was!

The second half of the morning was spent in reading aloud, painful and laborious business for many of the children, but Anna and a few more fluent readers were allowed to read in a group at their own speed, whilst Miss Stewart toiled with the others. The 'reading books' contained short stories, mainly fables, folk tales and fairy tales and after continual reading they became dull and boring.

After this there would be spelling, poetry, handwriting or 'composition' for the more able ones.

The last was Anna's favourite thing. Her imagination ran riot and she never had time to write it all down! She loved the frequently recurring themes: 'My Adventures, by a Penny,' 'The Life Story of a Dog, Horse, Cat.' There was no holding her back! The adventures those pennies had, the largesse they bestowed ... the cruel fates that overtook the animals ... these things were inexhaustible.

At the beginning of each term it was a foregone conclusion that the subject would be 'My holidays,' a subject met with sighs and groans for most, nay practically all, the children had 'Just been 'ome.' But once again Anna's tales of imaginary adventure and lovely leisure days at her beloved Greenfield, or of visits to relatives, enabled her most happily to cover several pages.

Elsie likewise enjoyed this theme for she had paid a visit to a city far removed from humble little Lowridge and her experience was unique.

An hour for dinner-break followed. The village children, and some from Rockyburn, scampered home; others from Rockyburn had brought meagre, unappetising scraps, often wrapped in newspaper or a none-too-clean piece of cloth, while the farm children enjoyed their thick cut wholesome sandwiches of bacon, cheese or home-made jam, washed down with pint cans of milk. They ate sitting at their desks or on the low wall at the back of the school. There was no supervision by the teachers, who either went home or clustered around the infants fire with their food and pot of tea brought in by the caretaker. In the coldest weather they would warm up the tins of tea or cocoa brought in by the children.

Anna was lucky for she could go to her married sister's in the village and play with the baby—her nephew!

The afternoon programme was less exciting, and needlework, drawing, football, singing, 'drill,' nature study, history and geography all had their turn.

Sometimes as a punishment older children were kept back after school to write out lines and it was not uncommon on winter afternoons for some of them to go home in the dark. It was very seldom that a parent complained—they were not over-protective of their young! On summer nights many children would stop to play around the village, sometimes for even two or three hours, till hunger drove them home. This too did not seem to cause any concern in their homes, unless they had been needed for any special reason and then 'a belting' would be awaiting them.

CHAPTER FIVE

LUCKY INFANTS

In the Infant's room a different atmosphere prevailed. Added to the main building some years after that had been built, the room was much brighter, with lower windows and none of the drab pitch pine, and brightly coloured nursery rhyme pictures covered walls. Better still, Miss Manley herself radiated brightness and cheerfulness among the little ones. She was a rather ungainly girl, not very good looking, dressed in somewhat tasteless and gaudy clothes and had a loud, hearty voice. But she was amazingly gentle if firm with the children—and they adored her! For she was full of fun, kind and completely fair. She could be relied on to sort out all their little problems, griefs and grievances with satisfaction all around. What was more, she could find something good, likeable and commendable in the dimmest, dirtiest and least attractive children. She glimpsed and encouraged 'promise' in the most unlikely little ones.

She could make the small boys and girls shout with laughter, sing with joyful if tuneless enthusiasm and could even put a skip into small feet shod in broken, ill-fitting boots.

Under her cheerful magic they learned their first lessons as perfectly as their mental endowment allowed. By the end of their third term most of them were reading the big-lettered wall charts which announced:

        IT IS AN OX.
        IS HE ON IT?
        NO, HE IS BY IT.
        THE PAN HAS A LID.
        MEG HAS A BAD LEG.
        BEG HER TO GET THE BAG.
        THE LASS IS ON THE ASS.
        THE BAD LAD HAD A WET CAP.

These and numerous other bits of tantalisingly incomplete and useless information, illustrated by, even then very old-fashioned, crudely coloured pictures, provided the children's first introduction into the realms of literature.

Plasticine worms and snakes, bird's nests and eggs grew under tiny fingers; innumerable beads were threaded, and not a few swallowed; coloured chalks for applying liberally to black paper—and faces—gradually turning into bright scenes of childish fancy; sticks and shiny counters were added and taken away with serious concentration.

A wet day provided the Infant's room odours and steam reminiscent of a railway tunnel. Miss Manley had the only open fire in school, the rest having hot-water pipes. There was no lack of coal for there were coal mines all around the district and the school was well supplied. So Miss Manley stoked up and the large brass-topped fireguard was draped and plugged with wet woollen stockings, often riddled with holes, shabby little overcoats and even shirts or dresses belonging to the coatless ones who had been caught in the downpour. Cracked and clumsy boots were arranged, soles uppermost, in rows inside the guard.

Still closer to the fire would be a few tin cans containing tea which Miss Manley 'stewed' till dinnertime.

"Johnnie Soper, can't your mother mend your stockings?" asks Miss Manley, holding up a practically footless object.

"No Miss, she 'asn't got'ny more safety pins—on'y these." Johnnie, big-eyed and serious, indicated two huge, dangerous-looking pins holding up his outsize trousers.

Most of such a morning was spent in turning and re-turning the wet garments while the children revelled in the warm fug, and wiggled none-too-clean little toes in the warmth, quite oblivious of the unsavoury odours arising from the seldom-washed, steaming clothes.

An old logbook of the school revealed that the problems of rainy days had not changed much in 30 years:

"… today we had a terrible rainstorm; only 30 pupils were present at 9 a.m. A few more came in at 10 a.m.—all very wet."

It continued: "… We must try to obtain a fireguard. It was so cold that the children could not sit in their places. I was obliged to let them go to the fire in groups."

Mr. Black seldom troubled Miss Manley. No doubt he realised her competence in coping with any problems in her domain; perhaps he recognised in her a rather formidable character prepared to defend her young at all costs!

On one memorable occasion he had come storming into her room, brandishing his cane and striking fear into many little hearts as he demanded to 'deal with' one of her small boys who had thrown soil down a drain.

"I have already dealt with him," said Miss Manley firmly, standing four-square between him and the timid culprit.

The Master blustered, his face darkening, and tried to pass her, but she stood her ground.

"Two punishments for one little offence?" she said, with a scornful lift of her dark eyebrows. "Even you must see the unfairness of that!" she said grimly.

Mr. Black's face was a picture of outraged astonishment. Never had any of his staff dared to question his authority. The whole room shuddered with the slam he gave the door as he retired, speechless and eyes popping.

Anna heard this story from her sister, who was friendly with Miss Manley. That lady had told the story with great enjoyment and eyes sparkling with mischief.

She did not live in Lowridge but daily cycled the two miles from Thickley where she was in lodgings, and where—it was darkly hinted among village gossips—she was 'too free with the boys.'

Whether that was true or not, she was a wonderful Infants' teacher and a true friend to several yearly intakes of children, some who received their first experience of real kindness and understanding from her, to say nothing of the sheer fun and joy in doing things that they had shared with her.

She had never been to college, her only training having been gained under a wise and enlightened headmistress in a distant town. She was classed as U.A.—uncertificated assistant—and probably received some £70 pounds a year, with no pay for holidays or sickness. Soon after the 1914 war broke out she joined up as a W.A.A.C., and neither Rockyburn nor Lowridge saw her again.

CHAPTER SIX

SCHOOL INTO CHURCH

The last hour of Friday afternoon was the nicest in the week in the opinion of most of the Big School—that is, from Standard 3 upwards. It was 'library time' when the children from Miss Stewart's room crowded into the big room, sitting with all their brothers and sisters or friends. A large cupboard unopened all week was now opened to disclose the 'liberry' books. Betty Butterfield was in charge, while the Master and Miss Stewart wrestled with the weekly summaries of the registers and any other clerical matters in the seclusion of the 'Oly Room.

The contents of the cupboard were arranged by some of Standard 7 on a long trestle table. Excitement mounted as the books were displayed. They ranged from fairy tales and animal stories with colour pictures, through a wide selection of 'Stent's Books for the Bairns,' the Fables of Aesop to the works of Lewis Carroll, Fenimore Cooper, Maryatt, Louisa M. Alcott and selections from Dickens. All except Stent's Books for the Bairns, which were very cheap, thin, paper-back books (but much loved), were uniformly backed in brown paper with titles in red ink. But this did not deter the keen readers, and there was much heart-burning as to who should have first pick.

It was not an easy task for Betty to make the choice for she wanted to please every child! But by and large she managed very well, varying the favourite ones from week to week, and seeing that those embarked on a book should have the chance to finish it. (She tried so hard not to favour Anna, who sometimes brought her a note from Steve!) As a special concession the most responsible older children were allowed to take a book home to finish, and the return of these was carefully checked.

When all the children were supplied silence reigned. To many of them this was their only access to literature, even the poorest readers liked to look at pictures and were glad to have this respite from ordinary and often boring routine. Sometimes Betty would take a little group of them into a corner and quietly read to them.

Anna was a voracious reader and had worked her way through all the younger children's selection and was now making good inroads into the older ones. Boy's books or girl's all were equally enjoyed, and the heroes of 'Deerslayer,' Jack, Ralph and Peterkin from 'Coral Island' and 'Midshipman Easy' were the companions of many an exciting adventure by the beckside and along the hedgerows of Greenfield.

At last the children were recalled from 'the dear land of storybooks,' and all except those to be taken home were safely locked away. Prayers were said and another week was over.

Then a transformation took place. The caretaker, who lived in a cottage a stone's throw away, came in. Assisted by three or four willing lads he began to set the scene for Sunday. They arranged the long four-seated desks into rows facing the small room which now came into its own as the chancel choir. The tops of the desks swung over and formed back rests. In the chancel the desks were made to face inwards and the floor between them was covered with red carpet. The Master's flat-topped desk, now covered with a snowy white cloth and embroidered frontal, was set out with two large brass candlesticks and a cross. All these and a pile of prayer books brought out from the mysterious cupboard. The simple lectern-pulpit was set in position on the top step, a large Bible was laid on it and School had become Church!

Anna and her brothers and sisters were regular attenders at the monthly service of Holy Communion at 9:15 a.m.— indeed they were frequently the only ones, as the villagers were not a devout lot by any means. Matins at 10:30 on the other Sundays was a little better and attended.

Anna enjoyed the liturgy, and the language of collects, canticles and psalms delighted her. She was thrilled afresh every time she heard the lovely *Te Deum*, a delight that was never to fade. Steve's sweet tender voice rang out and she paused in her own singing to listen and admire.

Often too, he read the lessons, and Anna would steal a look at Betty on the quiet to confirm her opinion that Betty was 'head over heels' about him. It bothered her sometimes —why didn't they 'go together!' Steve sent her notes, and she took back the replies … they just seem to be 'having each other on.' Oh, well, that was their way of courting, she thought, and they both seemed to enjoy the game.

The service over, home again often at a run, for farm chores have to be done on Sundays as well as weekdays. Some chores, that is. Anna's father, whose allegiance was to the Wesleyan Church, would allow only the absolute necessities to be performed. 'Six days shalt thou labour' was his Biblical command. However brightly the sun might shine he would never make hay on Sunday, nor indeed do any kind of fieldwork. Animals alone were to be tended. Nor was he alone in this respect, for few people in the country worked on Sunday whatever might be the restraining motive. When a neighbouring farmer's haystack burst into flames from internal combustion, the local verdict was unsympathetic. "Aye, well! What could y'expect? He led it o' Sunda!"

Sunday dinner was another matter and Anna's mother and one of the girls worked most of the morning to produce a huge and excellent meal. There would be a large joint of beef, pork or mutton, or a fowl to roast in the oven heated by the kitchen range, which seemed to devour coal and clumps of wood brought in from the woodpile. Lots of vegetables were prepared—from field or garden—flour, eggs, and milk vigorously beaten together to result in big, light fluffy Yorkshire puddings which were to form a complete first course! Rich gravy was poured off from the deliciously aroma'd meat joint and thickened, creamy sauces were stirred to mask the cauliflower, celery or broad beans, and parsnips and turnips mashed with a dash of butter. A luscious apple, rhubarb or plum pie, made earlier in the week, was eaten with cream from the dairy. Almost everything was home produced. Even the meat could well have been from their own sheep or cattle, for the butcher at Thickley was accustomed to buy from the farm.

For once in the week all the family could sit down together for the meal, so it was served in the dining room, the long table covered with a stiffly starched white damask cloth which almost touched the floor. Anna thought it was very elegant, and it seemed so right that Father should say grace! The elegance seemed to have its effect on the family for conversation was almost limited to "Pass the ... thanks ... yes, please ... mmm!" Or was it that the food was so good that it merited all one's attention?

Hardly was the dinner over when Anna was off again, alone this time, to Sunday School. The mile walk seemed as nothing for she would be meeting Elsie and a few more of her special friends and in the less 'religious' atmosphere of Sunday School they would have some light-hearted chatter and even some fun.

Usually the classes were taken by village women, and girls who had not long left school. The latter, having 'done' their Catechism so thoroughly at school and more recently for confirmation, liked to show off their superior knowledge, and 'went on and on' about it till they found themselves competing against the whispers and giggles of their pupils. There would also be Bible stories, or stories with morals, and now-and-then heart rending accounts of the 'poor little heathen children!'

There were only one or two hymns. As Anna and Elsie progressed at their music lessons they were sometimes called on to accompany the hymns—a great honour indeed! In spite of its ornately decorated 'pipes,' the organ in reality was only a simple harmonium with a very limited range of stops. At first the young organists' repertoire was also very limited. 'Art thou weary?' 'Sun of my soul,' and 'O God our help in ages past' were perhaps not very suitable for the tender ages of the singers. However, these supported their accompanists very loyally, lustily covering up their wrong notes or waiting till the right ones were found.

Anna liked it best of all when they were visited by the curate, a most jolly and kind and a wonderful teacher—and he was blind!

He read from a great Braille Bible which he let them touch and marvel over. He taught them so much that was new and arresting about the Christian faith. Even the usually restless and inattentive ones fell under his spell. He had a fund of stories both grave and gay and Bible stories took on an entirely new aspect when he told them. The well-known fields around the village became the setting for the parables of the sower, the good shepherd, the ox in the ditch; and Old Mokey, the donkey tethered on the green, the very one that carried Mary to Bethlehem or Jesus into Jerusalem.

He taught the children to stand smartly to attention when saying the Creed.

"In olden days," he said, "When men were persecuted for being Christians, a knight or soldier would stand to attention, hand on sword, ready to defend to the death his right to say what he believed."

This greatly appealed to the boys and unfortunately sometimes (but not when they curate was present) led to mock fights and irreverent miming which ended in the naughty lads being forcibly put out.

He told them the reason for the two candles on the altar. "One for the Godhead, one for the Manhood of Christ," they repeated after him, little understanding what it meant but eagerly waiting for him to choose who should be allowed to extinguish the candles.

In spite of their high spirited and sometimes unruly behaviour they really loved the blind curate and attendance was good, particularly when he was expected. It may have been too that the prospect of a Christmas party and a summer trip to the seaside for regular attenders had a marked effect on the attendance.

Often Anna would be invited to Elsie's home for tea and then she would go to Evensong and meet some of her family and have company home afterwards. She noticed that Steve did not return with them and almost always he would send a note to Betty next morning saying with a grin to Anna, "Just something I forgot to tell her last night."

Evensong was the most popular service, the day's chores being finished and most of the congregation—the men certainly—had had a 'lie-in' in the morning or a snooze in the afternoon. Now several of the uncomfortable pews were filled and choir seats occupied by a few well-scrubbed boys in their best navy-blue serge suits and cellulose collars, half a dozen young girls vying with one another in the matter of Sunday best clothes, and three or four older men and women. Anna sat with her sister and brother-in-law, who usually got someone to mind the baby. Sometimes her parents were there too having a change from the dingy little chapel in Rockyburn or not feeling like taking the long walk to Thickley. Steve, Hugh and Zilla were in the choir, but the two other sisters had opted for a long walk to the parish church where they had boyfriends who would not think the two miles too far to take the girls home, getting them there by 10 o'clock prompt!

Anna was parted from Elsie, for Elsie had the honour of being the youngest member of the choir, by reason of her sweet and cheerful voice.

Having had the vicar or curate in the morning the congregation had to be satisfied with the administrations of a lay preacher in the evening. Some of these were fine men of strong faith and zeal who would preach a sermon both interesting and uplifting. Others were uneducated, halting and uninspiring and the congregation shuffled impatiently or dozed until they were finished.

Mr. Black, who was choirmaster and organist, often read one of the lessons. His apparent godliness cut little ice with the schoolchildren. They would chant—well out of his hearing:

> "Mr. Black is a very good man,
> He goes to church o' Sunda',
> He prays that he will have the strength
> To whack the kids o' Monda' "

And Monday came around again with surprising speed, and low and behold it was school again, with Church 'put away' for another week, like the library books.

CHAPTER SEVEN

PLEASANT DIVERSIONS

"Please, I found this in our garden. Can you tell me what it is, sir?"

Scripture lesson was over and Mr. Black's class had reluctantly got out their slates and books in preparation for arithmetic. The Friday test had been badly done and they were expecting some unpleasantness.

Jim Croft, a bright faced thirteen-year-old, produced from under his desk a jam-jar half-full of leaves and flowers to which a lovely moth was clinging.

The stern face of the master became as bright and eager as the boy's as he examined the small creature carefully. If there was one thing could change his habitual grimness it was 'nature' and the children knew this and took every opportunity of profiting by it. It could mean a digression into any lesson and there were occasions when a digression meant the avoidance of some unpleasantness. Even a much dreaded and imminent caning was known to have been sidetracked and actually forgotten.

"A rare find, Jim!" he explained with enthusiasm. "Nothing less than a hummingbird hawk-moth. Did you notice anything particular about its movements before you caught it?"

"Why yes, sir—it sort of hovered like a sparra'hawk, over the tobacco flowers."

"Yes! Yes! A good description. And that's a flower it favours!" He was getting warmed up. The class waited, legs swinging happily.

"Put away your sum books," ordered the Master, a command that did not need repeating. "We'll see what we can learn about *Lepidoptera*. Jim, run across to my house and ask Mrs. Black to give you Volume 6 of my Natural History Encyclopaedias."

Jim was soon back and an interesting lesson was under way. Coloured pictures were passed round, excellent blackboard diagrams drawn and the life cycle the moth unfolded like a thrilling story. Enthusiasm mounted.

"Please, sir, I seen one like that!" Bobby Clay shouted excitedly as he picked out the picture of rare type.

"You haven't!" incredulously from Mr. Black.

"Yes sir! God's truth!"

Even this blasphemous expression was overlooked in the light of his incredible claim.

"I'll give you a shilling if you could show it to me, Clay!"

A shilling! Riches untold! And Bobby knew it was as good as in his pocket for the Master never broke a promise and Bobby knew just where that moth was! It was impaled on his bedroom wall, and had been waiting there for just such an opportune moment. It took but a few minutes to fetch it, and as it was indeed the moth of the picture the Master's promise was honoured.

The crowning point of the lesson was reached when a master gave out sheets of paper, some precious dabs of watercolour paints and brushes and let the children make copies of his drawings and some of the gorgeously coloured pictures in his book. Then—who would've believed it!—it was dinnertime and they never thought of sums or grammar; they never even missed playtime—and no one had asked to leave the room!

Jim and Bobby were the heroes of the hour and received much backslapping. Johnny Craggs, who had escaped certain chastisement due on account of his 'none right' test, gratefully pressed on Jim the remains of the sticky mint humbug which had been gathering a fine covering of fluff and grass seed from residing in his pocket between surreptitious sucks. But, to do them justice, the children had greatly enjoyed the lesson for its own sake, for Mr. Black's enthusiasm for nature study was genuine and he had the art of getting it across.

One of his most popular traits was his habit of unexpectedly switching over to a subject other than that on the timetable. He had frequently been known to abandon a history lesson for which he had little liking. There was no regret in the class over this, for history invariably meant reading round the class a paragraph each of tedious accounts of Long Parliaments, Magna Carter and suchlike, considered suitable for 'top classes.' They had already, by the end of Standard 4, read or heard all the racy titbits from the past, such as Alfred and the cakes; William the Red, shot in the head; Bruce and the spider; Drake and the game of bowls and the like. They had looked at all the pictures in 'Highroads to History' and had little further interest in the subject.

One memorable occasion occurred when Mr. Black threw England's constitutional problems to the winds, or rather the sunshine—for it was a radiant golden afternoon glowing with the late sunshine that would soon be only a memory. A short talk about seed dispersal, and then they were off, armed with paper bags, to make a collection of ripening fruits and seed-boxes in a small wood not far from the village. Almost two hours later, as the rest of the school was being dismissed, they returned, glowing with the sun and with happiness but with only a few acorns, hips and haws. They had soon chanced on a fox's earth with some delightful cubs playing around. So they had sprawled, squatted or knelt like so many statues, watching their charming antics until pins-and-needles had attacked first one and then another and their unavoidable groans and stretching had frightened the cubs away. To ease his conscience for what might have been construed as time-wasting the Master kept them in for half an hour to copy the set of notes on autumn fruits, which they did without a single sigh or grumble. Joseph Barnes, a small farmer's son with a long walk home, whispered to his desk mate, "I'll get a beltin' from me Da for not gettin' home in time for milkin'—but I don't care. It was worth it to see them bonnie little cubses."

It was not only his own classes that reaped the benefit of Mr. Black's penchant for switching lessons. When the mood seized him to go into another class, he would set his own children to trace maps. They did this with meticulous care, breathing heavily as they put in every little wiggle and bend of the coastline; rivers starting thin as hair and broadening out splendidly as they neared the sea; mountains shaded feather-light and looking like hairy caterpillars. The name of every namable feature had to be printed minutely with the proper mapping pens. Even some of the least intelligent could shine at this. The children new to this art were allowed to trace round shapes of Australia, Africa and India presumably because of their wiggle-free outlines. There was little fear of idleness in his absence.

The timetable told him that Standard 4 were ready to 'do' poetry, and for poetry Mr. Black had a love equalled only to his love of nature study and singing, so to Miss Stewart's room he made his way.

Standard 3 were busy embarked on writing out spellings and Miss Stewart had just written on the blackboard: 'The Daffodils' by William Wordsworth.

The children were waiting, lethargically for the most part, for her to begin. Her usual method was to read the poem through to them. She would then write on the board such words and phrases that she assumed needed explaining. After extracting a few wild guesses from the children as to their meanings, she would give the correct ones, by which time the pupils had lost what little interest the first reading had aroused. Then she read the first verse, next getting them to repeat it after her line by line. By the time they had done this two or three times most of them could gabble through the first verse. The remaining verses would be learnt in a similar manner in following poetry lessons till the whole poem was learnt.

But today Mr. Black had arrived in time to halt this mutilation.

"Now, Miss Stewart," he began breezily, "I see you are going to take the children for a beautiful spring walk by a lake. Well, just you sit down and I'll take them. Standard 3 can come as well if they like." (They did.)

Miss Stewart, blushing furiously, partly with resentment and partly because she knew she merited his implied criticism of her dull method, took her chair into a corner.

Eyes brightened, little faces came 'alive' as the Master led them and two friends, William and Dorothy, from lovely little Dove Cottage, through bluebell woods (there was one of these not far away and most of the children had seen it in its glory), out into the open where white, billowy clouds floated lazily among the mountain tops. (None of them had seen a mountain but they'd seen pictures of them.) And there before them lay a great yellow carpet of daffodils by a sparkling blue lake! "Fluttering and dancing, those daffodils were," he said. "Flutt-er-ing and dancing," he said over and over again, gently, staccato, rhythmically bringing out the dancing quality of the words. At the flick of his finger the children joined in, swinging their legs and smiling: "Fluttering and dancing," till it was almost a song.

Bit by bit he introduced words and phrases, in a way unobtrusively giving the meaning and adding to their meagre vocabulary, and when he felt they had had enough of this he read the whole poem. There was a long happy sigh as he closed the book.

"Playtime," he said briskly and the children filed out quite quietly.

A few minutes later he looked out of the window and saw two little girls holding their skirts and tripping round in an improvised dance while they sang, "Fluttering and dancing *in* the breeze."

"I think you should read them some of the Burns poems," he said with mischievous twinkle. "How about 'To a mouse,' or 'My love is like a red, red rose'—they'd love it in an authentic accent."

"But they wouldn't understand it," protested Miss Stewart indignantly.

"What matter? They'd enjoy it. They'd probably laugh too. Poetry is meant to be enjoyed, Miss Stewart—didn't you know?"

Miss Stewart bridled slightly. "Well, I think it's a waste of time to read something so far beyond their comprehension."

"Well, so was 'Daffodils,' wasn't it?"

Anyway, she tried, giving the Scottish words their native pronunciation, but alas! there was no music nor inspiration in her reading so she failed to get the response the Master had hoped for. All that happened was a good deal of nudging and giggling.

"Funny, wasn't it?" Anna said as they went home.

"Funny!" returned Elsie scornfully. "It was daft!"

Anna grew to love poetry and delighted in the Master's unconventional way of presenting it. Perhaps he felt it was a way of bringing some joy and beauty to the lives of these children, mostly so lacking in culture of any kind. His interruptions of geography, history and deadly dull formal lessons in English to be replaced by poetry became more frequent as he realized that Miss Stewart lacked the necessary spark. He dreaded the effect that she would have on those few receptive little spirits that he recognized throughout the school.

Miss Manley's jolly, racy jingles and nursery rhymes had been a good and happy introduction to poetry and Betty Butterfield had followed these up with verses by Ann and Jane Taylor and from 'A Child's Garden of Verse,' but there was nothing else for it—he would teach the rest of the school himself. At his own expense, augmenting the meagre allowance for books, he bought some sets of anthologies and a few copies of more advanced ones, including Palgrave's 'Golden Treasury' for older children.

As with the library books, Anna was soon to dip into the latter. They had it at home too, so she was not a complete stranger to it. Steve used to read poetry with her—he had got a taste for it at grammar school. He was actually reading 'Marmion' to her!

With Anna, to read was to remember and she memorized poem after poem saying them aloud as she went to and from school through the fields. She often kept the 'Golden Treasury' under her desk for a secret read when she could. Many of the poems were far beyond her understanding but touched some chord of response by their beauty as did the words of the Church's liturgy.

"Can you say your favourite one for me?" asked Mr. Black one wet playtime when he found Anna reading Palgrave while the other children noisily played at noughts and crosses on their slates.

"Well, sir, I like such a lot," she laughed. "But this is a nice one," she said. She repeated with obvious enjoyment 'When icicles hang by the wall,' followed with 'Spring, the sweet Spring' by Nashe, fitting the words to a lilting sing-song and involuntary swaying to the rhythm.

"I love 'The Forsaken Merman,' but it's so long, I only know a few lines of it," she said. "I like the bit where it says something like:

'Through the surge and through the swell

Down swung the sound of the far-off bell.' "

Mr. Black laughed with pure delight—a rare sound.

"I never got better value for anything I ever bought," he said enigmatically as he tapped her on the head gently with the 'Golden Treasury.'

CHAPTER EIGHT

AN IMPORTANT DAY

In the middle of the spring term Scripture suddenly assumed tremendous importance, and for a week or two the lessons were lengthened out well into the time allotted to arithmetic. The sing-song repetition of the Ten Commandments, the Creed and the Catechism could be heard throughout the school. Betty Butterfield was kept busy at the piano as each class in turn practiced the chosen hymns. Then the classes would be united and Mr. Black would take over.

Not only did the children learn many hymns relating to the Church's year bit they learned to sing them *well* and in two-part harmony. The parts were written in tonic solfa, on a large wall-chart, Betty coming in early in the morning or staying behind after school to do this very tedious task. Trebles and altos learned each other's parts so that they could change as required. When one hymn was satisfactory it was erased from the chart and another took its place.

They learned the meanings of 'cresc.,' 'dim.,' 'p,' 'f' and many other musical terms and sang with much enjoyment and not a little pride as a rule. Another accomplishment which Mr. Black skilfully taught was the chanting of psalms and even the little ones not long out of the Infant's department could chant the 23rd Psalm.

So satisfactory, pleasing and unusual was was this part of the religious teaching that an inspector a few years previously wrote in his report:

"The chanting of psalms and the harmonized singing of hymns was very good, and in the Infant's division the singing deserves special note, the chanting of a psalm being excellent for such young children."

And on one of the rare occasions when the school received a visit from Lady V—its most esteemed manageress —the children so charmed her with their singing that Mr. Black entered her gratifying comment in the log book: "I have never in any school heard such sweet singing from children."

Something to live up to, indeed. However, to achieve this standard much pain and grief had to be endured, in the initial stages at least. Unfortunately, the Master's love of music had not the humanizing effect on him as had nature study and poetry. A jarring note, a loud rendering of a soft passage could send him into one of his frightening rages. He would yell and slap the desk with his cane and go round among the scared children, head bent to their mouth-level, listening for a false note. Then—thump!—his hand would land in the middle of some small, thinly-clad back and he would bawl angrily at the miserable little culprit.

Jackie Tarn, not very bright but aware of his tunelessness, made all the correct shapes with his mouth but uttered not a sound, hoping thus to escape the thumps. Alas for his simple strategy! The Master was too old a bird to be caught with such chaff; nor did he pity Jackie's simplicity but gave him an extra thump for trying to deceive.

All this effort was leading up to the bi-annual scripture examination to be conducted by a reverend gentleman from the Diocesan Religious Education Board.

Was this what made the Master so irritable and violent? So much depended on the report he would get. A Headmaster had been known to be downgraded for his poor report; a man's promotion to a bigger church school stood little chance if the religious teaching in his school did not reach a high enough standard; on the other hand an excellent report could be the deciding factor in a promotion. Enough to make a man angry and nervous?

On the day before the examination the children were carefully briefed. They were earnestly admonished to take a bath and have their hair washed. In the middle of the week! But everyone knows that Friday is bath night! But all the same they mostly obeyed, and oddly enough none of the parents was at all put out by this outrageous suggestion, for they had all gone through it themselves.

The boys were to have their hair brushed and neatly parted. (They said they would use plenty of 'tap-oil.') Their celluloid collars were to be clean and their boots polished well. Some who were fortunate enough to possess them might be asked to be allowed to wear their Sunday suits.

Anna and Elsie and a few more of the really lucky ones had Saturday dresses as well as Sunday ones, and these they wore with much pride and preening.

On the great day they all assembled for lines self-consciously and subdued, knowing that 'he'd come.' It was pathetic to see the attempt that had been made by the poorest children to rise to the occasion, clean hair and faces being the greatest improvement, and some had managed to cover their shabby dresses with a clean pinafore.

The inspector was waiting beside the Master, and greeted them kindly.

Prayers were said and the hymn sung with unusual restraint, and then they breathlessly awaited the verdict—who was to be the first for the fray? It was uncertain which was the lesser of the two evils—whether to be the first and get it over, or to sit anxiously awaiting one's turn.

Well, it was Infants first. Their examination did not take very long. They sang sweetly 'Loving Shepherd of The Sheep,' two verses of 'We are but little children weak,' and said the Lord's Prayer. 'Volunteers,' well-briefed by Miss Manley, came out to the front to tell in sections a story from their Bible repertoire.

'Adamaneve' was a favourite, and translated into the little one's own language (for they had freedom in this) could be very entertaining.

Little cross-eyed Billy Foster took over where Sarah Tate left off. He rolled his eyes alarmingly, drew a big breath and began gruffly.

"So God saw Adamaneve a-back o' the bushes an' He said, 'Come on out o' there, you two. I can see what yer upter!'"

"That's enough, thank you Billy," intervened Miss Manley, swiftly and tactfully.

"Eve was made out of spare-rib," brightly explained Clive Green, who father killed and cured pigs and had carefully taught Clive the names of all the cuts.

"I think we had better sing another hymn," the reverend judiciously decided after he had heard a dramatic account of David 'hoyin' (throwing) a great big styan (stone) at t'giant.' So Miss Manley sat down the rather tinny piano ('good enough for Infants') and they sang lustily and unafraid 'Onward Christian Soljers.'

"And now," said the great man kindly, and with a twinkle that had been discretely restrained until now, "You've been very good and done well in your stories and singing so you may all have a holiday and go home."

The little ones had been told to expect this but perhaps the excitement of the examination had driven it out of their thoughts so now they gasped with genuine surprise and one or two of the daring gave a little clap. But Billy Foster burst into tears.

"I don wanter go 'ome," he wailed. "Me Ma'll make me put me old clo's on again, an' I like these."

He smoothed his new outsize corduroy trousers lovingly and big tears dropped on his shiny boot toes.

So thorough had been the teaching in the Master's own classes that the examiner cut short his oral examination after a bare half hour, well pleased with the response. Hands had shot up eagerly to answer the questions on the Catechism, memory work was faultless and the Bible stories well known. So he left the top classes writing out their favourite parable— or was it one they had written so often, 'just in case'—whilst he went to the lower standards.

The latter having acquitted themselves reasonably well, all were gathered to sing some prepared hymns.

"Three selected hymns were sung beautifully: Psalm 121 rendered with precision and feeling," his report said.

Then the inspector announced what they were all waiting for—holiday for the rest of the day. Broad grins spread around and there was a small burst of clapping quickly subdued by Mr. Black, who said they would bring the session to an end with another hymn.

And now the children let themselves go with joyful abandon. Forgotten were all the 'pp-s,' the 'dims,' 'rall-s' and 'cresc-s' so painfully learnt; 'ff' was the order of the day, and the black clouds gathering ominously on the Master's face were nonchalantly ignored. For the holiday was assured—even *he* could not stop that—and had they not just been saying:

'Take no thought for the morrow?'

CHAPTER NINE

SCOTCH BROTH

"I'm going to ask Miss Stewart to tea next Saturday," Anna smugly informed Elsie one sunny playtime as the two sat swinging their legs on the low stone wall that ran round the back of the school. It was skipping time and marble time, but Anna had been hinting all morning that she had a secret to impart so they had withdrawn to this comparatively quiet spot to make the most of her announcement.

Elsie was duly impressed—flabbergasted in fact.

"You're *not!*"

One didn't *dare* ask a teacher to tea!

"I am, so there! Our Philip's coming home for the weekend and he wants to see her about something important."

Elsie made big eyes at her friend and grinned mischievously and they both began to giggle.

"Is he going to ask her to marry him?" asked Elsie through her giggles.

"Pooh! He'd better not," Anna groaned and made a face. "She's all right at school but I wouldn't like her for a sister. She's is far over bossy."

Elsie agreed wholeheartedly.

"Nobody would want scotch broth everyday," she said thereby hitting a nickname that stuck, and set off the giggles again.

Miss Stewart was still regarded as an 'incomer' in Lowridge although she had been there for three years. To the insular villagers anyone who had not been born there or within a radius of about ten miles was a 'foreigner' and Miss Stewart came from *Scotland!* She lived with her sister and brother-in-law who had bought 'Holmlands,' the most prosperous farm in the district. They had little to do with the village folk, but made their friends among higher circles.

Occasionally in the worst weather the young farmer would drive his sister-in-law to school in the pony-trap, but usually she cycled or walked. She was twenty-four when she first came, a good-looking girl who wore attractive clothes and spoke with a pleasant not too strong Scottish accent. In spite of these attractions, however, she was never very popular. She had been educated at a very good school and collage, facts which she let fall too often for the local folk's liking! Her accent, at first a source of amusement to the village people, was copied by a few of the oldest girls who secretly admired and envied her. Elsie was not one of her admirers.

"Do you remember the day I kicked her on the shins?" chuckled the naughty Elsie.

"Ooh yes! I'll never forget it!" squealed her friend. "Eee! You *were* awful!"

The incident had occurred during a history lesson. Mary Queen of Scots and her tribulations at the hands of the English Elizabeth had been the subject, and there was a decided bias on the part of Miss Stewart toward her fellow country-woman. Elsie could stand it no longer, and no doubt spurred on by the fact that she had been kept in at playtime for some misdemeanour, she shouted out:

"She was a horrid, bad Queen!" to the amazement of everyone, herself included.

"Come out, you impudent, saucy girrrl! I'll sorrrt you!" cried the indignant teacher, using her direst threat.

Elsie sauntered out, giving her blond ringlets a haughty, don't care toss, while the class held their breath in shocked but joyful anticipation.

"You apologise at once," said Miss Stewart grimly gripping Elsie by the shoulders and giving her a shaking.

"I'm sorry for shouting it out," said Elsie demurely, then she added quickly, "But I'm not sorry for old Mary Scot—so there!"

In her excitement she jerked away from Miss Stewart's grip and her foot shot forward, catching the teacher a sharp blow on the shin which made her call out with the shock and pain.

There was a note to Elsie's parents with the account of her 'insolence and rudeness' and they made Elsie apologize all over again, which she did in her most 'ladylike' way, taking a bunch of flowerers to help things along.

From that day, Miss Stewart and Elsie, though never exactly friendly, treated one another with a rather wary respect. Elsie was particularly impressed and grateful for the fact that 'Scotch Broth' hadn't told Mr. Black about her. Miss Stewart perhaps appreciated the fact that at least one pupil was sufficiently attentive in her history lessons to disagree with her!

The Saturday visit to Anna's home did not after all materialize, for Miss Stewart developed a sore throat on Friday afternoon and sent a note via Anna to excuse herself. So Philip's question remained unasked.

The two friends, feeling very noble and charitable after Sunday School on the following day, decided that they would walk across the fields to Holmlands to enquire after Miss Stewart, take her a bunch of flowers and incidentally show off their Sunday finery. They hoped, nay, they were sure they would be asked to tea in the parlour, for that, they understood, was where Miss Stewart was accustomed to have tea. There would be a lace tablecloth, a silver teapot, real china cups and lovely cakes!

It was a beautiful, hot day in early June and they were wearing white, well-stretched 'embroidery' dresses with pink and blue sashes respectively, Anna a daisy-decked, and Elsie a poppy wreathed Leghorn straw hat. Both wore white socks and shiny, black patent-leather 'low' shoes—a great refinement, for black, buttoned boots were normal wear. They felt equal to taking tea with royalty.

It was a long walk over the fields in spite of the short cuts they took. The golden pollen of the long grasses and buttercups dusted their shoes and socks; they gathered red campions and marsh marigolds and forget-me-nots by a stream, and Elsie mistaking a slab of mud for a stone stepped in. One leg was soaked and caked in mud almost up to her knee. Anna, in trying to break a spray of delicate green beech leaves, stumbled against the tree trunk and made a big black smudge down the front of her dress. She had already lost a hair-ribbon and one plait was undone. They were hot, very thirsty and not a little dispirited, so they sat down for a rest. On rising each exclaimed dismay at the other's grass-stained seat.

It was a dishevelled and disheartened little couple that eventually arrived at Holmlands. And now they suddenly turned shy, realizing that if Miss Stewart was confined to bed, one of her relatives would likely come to the door. They knew well enough too, that the village folk would say they were a 'stuck-up lot.' However, they had come a long way and suffered much, so plucking up courage they advanced with a look of grim determination on their heat-stained little faces, and knocked on the imposing oak front door.

After a terribly long minute the door was opened by a tall, gaunt woman in a black dress, white cap and apron. She glared at them unsmilingly.

"Please," faltered Anna, "We've come to see how Miss Stewart is, and we've brought her these." Each little girl held out a droopy assortment of wild flowers, leaves and grasses.

"Och aye," said the gaunt one, in a tone that conveyed a complete lack of interest, and took the flowers with a limp, unwilling hand.

The girls waited uncomfortably. Then, "How is she?" asked Elsie with none of her usual self-assurance.

"Och, she's no sae bad," said the woman. "I'll tell her ye speired." She shut the door.

Anna and Elsie turned away. They looked at one another and hastily looked away again; they were too near to tears to speak. It was such a long way from home. They were both parched with thirst and hadn't even had the chance to ask for a drink of water. Besides, they were in no doubt about what their mothers would have to say about the site of their clothes.

However, after their almost silent trudge home, when they told their sad tale to Elsie's mother, she was so outraged with the shabby treatment the children had met with that their appearance was overlooked—for the time being—and they were consoled with jelly, bread and butter, rice cake and jam tarts—a most delicious tea, albeit eaten only in a humble cottage kitchen.

Miss Stewart never referred to the visit, so the girls concluded that the 'long string of misery' had not told her that they had 'speired'—whatever that might mean!

CHAPTER TEN

KITH AND KIN

As is usual in many small villages, there was a good deal of intermarrying in Lowridge, a regular network of relationships, close and distant, resulting. Tracing their links back to their beginnings, usually with the aid of a family Bible, was like finding 'which cat gets the mouse?' in a children's puzzle maze. The feuds, petty jealousies, bickering and back-biting that were rife were more often than not among related families. But in cases of trouble such as illness, accident or death the sufferers could always count on the support of these self-same relatives! 'Our Emma' or 'Our John' would rally round at once —the prefix always denoting some degree of kinship however remote.

Jennie and Mollie Clay were second cousins who had married two brothers. The four had known each other all their lives so there were few secrets among them, but it was incredible how either woman could rake up some unsavoury bit of scandal from the past to confound the other when they were indulging in one of their periodic 'dust-ups.'

"Ask your Jim why he got the sack at Pear Tree Farm," taunted Jennie in one of these rows.

"Sack!" screamed her sister-in-law. " 'E left t'better hisself. 'E gets twice as much at Holmlands." A regretful slip of the tongue that Mollie realized too late.

"Oh! 'E does, does 'e? Then mebbe you'll pay me that five bob you borrowed with your 'ard up tales, weeks back."

Bursting with indignation, Mollie rushed away to her own house, returning five minutes later with the money, fully intending to fling it dramatically, with a suitable epithet, at Jennie's feet.

But Jennie was stretched out unconscious on the stone kitchen floor, having had one of her 'dizzy fits.' She had hit her head on the edge of the steel fender and it was bleeding freely. Mollie, big and buxom, heaved her onto the settle and did her best to staunch the wound. She got the next door neighbour in (though they were not on speaking terms at the moment) and together they put the sufferer to bed and sent to Thickley for the doctor.

By the time he arrived Jennie had come round and was having a cup of tea while Mollie sat on the bed gently supporting her!

"I think you'd better get your mother to come and look after you for a few days," suggested Dr. Smith, who knew all the family history and was well aware of the women's quarrels. Indeed he'd not have been surprised if they'd had a real fight and Mollie had knocked out her sister-in-law.

Jennie protested peevishly. "Our Mollie'll look after me, won't you Moll?"

"Why of course, Jinny," said her ex-enemy, giving her a clumsy hug and looking at the doctor with scorn.

"No need to send for t'old woman. What's to stop me tending 'er—we're sisters-'i-law, aren't we?"

A funeral always brought a gathering of the clans in sombre black clothes that were hopelessly old-fashioned, as they were preserved carefully over the years for such occasions. There was much whispering and nudging when some relative, unheard of for years, turned up out of the blue, and expressions of sympathy with the bereaved did not ring very true after a lifetime of petty quarrels. A will, however small, stirred up animosities old and new.

One day as Elsie and Anna came out of school, Elsie's aunt met them with a grim, tight-lipped look.

"Don't call at Uncle Jack's today," she said curtly.

Uncle Jack, extremely distantly connected by a labyrinth of marriages, was a nice old man whom the girls often visited, running errands for him and listening to his rambling stories of this youth. A further attraction was an ancient parrot which fascinated them with its wide vocabulary.

"What for?" demanded Elsie imperiously.

"He's dead."

"He's *not!*" shouted Elsie in disbelief.

"Yes he is, you bad girl—don't you contradict your elders," retorted her aunt, giving Elsie a smart slap.

The girls were upset at the loss of their old friend and not a little touched when it was found that he had, apparently just before he died, managed to scribble on a bit of paper:

"I leave Polly (the parrot) to my little Frend Ellie Dent and the kage. Sined, Jack BAILEY."

Uncle Jack's older sister, who turned up at the funeral from regions unknown, had other ideas and insisted that she have Polly and cage. That wise old bird fortunately solved the problem by dying as suddenly as her master had done, and as Elsie had no use for the 'kage' the old woman took it away in triumph, nevertheless muttering darkly about people that would even steal an old man's bird, and managing to convey that they had in some way brought about its end.

Elsie was proud of her two aunts who lived in the village. In their late twenties they were unmarried and looked after their widowed mother, Elsie's grandma, and their small general shop which supplied most of the simple wants of the villagers, in the way of groceries, haberdashery, sweets and basic household utensils. It was one of Elsie's great treats to dole out half-penny-worths of sherbet, liquorice 'bootlaces,' lucky bags and pear drops to those fortunate children who had a 'Saturday penny' to spend.

The business did well and the aunts, who were clever at dressmaking, were continually appearing in new and stylish garments to the envy of the other young women. Both were in the church choir and one could be sure that if they were late they would arrive in new clothes, making their way up to the choir seats with self-conscious preening. They usually looked quite attractive but their rather silly vanity seemed to put off the young men as far as romance was concerned.

The two young ladies were, however, crazy about tennis and never lacked male partners at the game. Behind the high wall of the one big house was a pleasant, well kept grass court which the owner, a retired colliery manager, had given for the use of the village. It was a very exclusive little club that appropriated it, consisting of some seven or eight

Lowridgers, two or three young farmers and half a dozen enthusiasts from Thickley, the latter by special invitation. The young people from Thickley, on Saturdays and evenings throughout the summer, walked the two dusty miles, played tennis with zest and vigour till the light faded, and then sauntered back talking over the games with untiring enthusiasm.

The two sisters were extremely good players and no match was played without them. They sprang lightly on the soft green turf in their white 'sandshoes' and long full-skirted white dresses, with slim waists tightly belted and strong arms discreetly covered.

Few children were allowed within the semi-sacred court, so Elsie considered it a tremendous favour to be taken in by her aunts and allowed to watch a match—better still when they said she might bring Anna too, for then the two friends would sit proudly on the steps of the pavilion and dream of the day when they might even be allowed to play.

It was bliss when they were asked to help in handing round the teas which were a pleasant gesture of the club's Saturday activities. The fresh scent of the newly mown grass, the ping of well-strung rackets, the chink of tea cups, the fragrant tea and dainty iced buns and biscuits from the aunts' shop were rare delights that Elsie bestowed generously on her friend, by virtue of her relationship with the club's two most ardent and indispensable supporters.

Relations had their good points after all.

CHAPTER ELEVEN

MORE KITH AND KIN

Anna's relations were of a different nature and their visits to the farm were greeted with varying degrees of pleasure.

"Your Aunt Sophie wants to come for a few days," said their mother one autumn morning after the postman had been. "She's not been very well. Father will have to go for her; you can go with him on Saturday if you like, Anna."

This was quite pleasant if not very exciting. Aunt Sophie, one of Mother's numerous elderly sisters, lived in a colliery village about six miles away. She was a widow and spent her days among her various married children and their families. As all of them were very poorly-off and as all had large families Aunt Sophie had a tiring and unpeaceful existence. Whenever she could stand the din and chaos no longer she would escape to Greenfield for a breather.

Saturday came round. Father harnessed the pony to the dog-cart and, rugs round their knees against the chilly wind, they trotted away for the visitor.

It was lovely jog-trotting along the lanes—first the twisty-turns one that led from the farm in a direction opposite to Lowridge. This was a narrow track with two parallel grassy ridges dividing the wheel tracks from those made by the horse's hooves. Often a rabbit would bunny-hop over these ridges almost under the pony's feet, or a pheasant rise up with a whirr of wings.

There was a huge holly bush with a plank concealed high up amidst the prickly, glossy leaves. This was the gamekeepers' look-out post where they sat after dusk watching for poachers, for the farm was part of the Whinstone Estate and the game was jealously guarded. Soon they were out on the real road, but it too was narrow and rough surfaced, and bordered by big hedges. There was very little traffic—the odd farm cart, pony-trap, butcher's van and a cyclist or two. The only car one would see would most certainly be the doctor's.

Anna and her father did not talk very much, but now and then he would point out something she might have missed—a fox skulking behind a barn, a weasel snaking along in the ditch and a squirrel drey high up in a beech tree.

At last they reached the mining village with long, narrow rows of shabby, back-to-back houses, their back yards strung with washing lines, and swarming with noisy, poorly-clad children. Although on the very edge of such pleasant country there was no sign of gardens, trees, grass or open spaces, and the pit-head with its huge winding gear, and backed by its ugly waste tip, loomed over all.

Aunt Sophie was eagerly awaiting their arrival in one of these streets. Her luggage, a basket-type of holder, known as a Japanese hamper, was already on the doorstep, while she sat by the window in her outdoor clothes, eagerly watching for their approach.

Anna and her father were invited into the little 'front room' and given a welcome cup of hot tea while a bunch of grubby little cousins-once-removed stood and gaped at them till they dispersed to squabble over the sack of apples that great-uncle Tom had brought, and to offer timidly a lump of sugar to the pony.

It was a bit of a problem getting Aunt Sophie up into the trap for she weighed fifteen stone and was not agile in consequence. Anna was both amused and embarrassed as her relations crowded round—observed by several interested neighbours—to assist Grandma into the front seat beside the driver. Anna had now transferred to the back with the luggage. The shafts creaked ominously and the pony shuffled impatiently, but at last after narrowly missing two of the youngsters, they were homeward bound. Aunt Sophie heaved a huge sigh of relief as the last yelled goodbye died away.

Removed from the overwhelming atmosphere of her family she was a cheery soul and good company. She had a hearty laugh, which was infectious as she entertained them all at the farm. She had a fund of stories of her homely doings;

what she had said to the vicar; how she threw the rent collector out of the house; why she changed her doctor and so on. All these anecdotes she told in a witty, good-natured way, for in spite of the hard life she had always known she was the soul of kindness and bore no-one ill will.

"What are you going to read us, Tom?" she asked on her second night. On several of her visits he had read aloud selections of tales from 'The Wide World Magazine' and 'The Quiver,' two favourite publications, to her great pleasure, for, once an avid reader, she could no longer see well enough.

"Oh, I've got a grand book for you, Sophie," he said readily as he had been expecting this request. It was 'David Copperfield.'

Anna's father was a good reader with a pleasant voice and a natural way for interpreting the spirit of the book. In the cosy big kitchen those of the family who were not out on their own pursuits for the evening gathered round to listen. Mother was mending from a basketful of wooden stockings; Anna sat on the hearth-rug with her arms round Roc, the collie; Aunt Sophie overflowed the rocking chair and the story unfolded. Anna's bedtime was often forgotten and supper was very late as night after night the reading continued, the only interruptions being Aunt Sophie's 'oh-s,' 'ee-s,' 'fancy that!' and similar interjections.

The few days she'd come for lengthened into a week, ten days, a fortnight.

"I'll have to go home," she would say with a sigh each morning, but at the sight of the fascinating book lying on the dresser, she would say, "Well, just one more chapter." And so she stayed, five weeks in all, in what they afterwards referred to as 'the David Copperfield visit.' She worked hard, helping with the huge bakings, washing-days, washing up and cleaning, and was so obviously happy that they were quite sad to see her go.

Sometimes when she came in the spring or summer for a shorter stay some of her family would descend unexpectedly —'just to see how she was'—but in reality for a day out and a good feed at the farm.

Two married daughters, their husbands and six children arrived one Easter Monday. They had had a lift for part of the way and had walked the rest so their appetites were truly whetted for the high-tea that was laid on for them. Home-fed bacon, eggs, stacks of bread and butter and home-made jam disappeared as if by magic, then the six children dispersed to wreak havoc among the poultry and animals in the farmyard. Anna had nothing in common with this unruly mob and kept her distance, even offering to wash up. She was greatly relieved when they all departed, having arranged for a 'waggonette' to pick them up at the lane end.

Another aunt was a regular summer visitor. This was father's sister, a prim and proper 'old maid' she was a nursery governess and companion in a well-to-do family at Newcastle.

Although the distance was only some forty miles, train connections were not very reliable so the time taken was ridiculously long and when Aunt Mary was met at the station with the pony-trap she was in a state of exhaustion and had to be cosseted and pampered for the next twenty-four hours.

After that she was ready to enjoy herself, with the family dancing attendance when they could not escape. The older ones had all gone through it and now it was Anna's turn, sometimes helped out by Zilla, who was not well enough to do much of the routine work of the household.

Aunt May, after breakfast in bed, would come downstairs ready for her holiday pleasures to begin. It would be, "You must show me the calves/foals/lambs that have been born since last summer ... You must walk to the village with me to buy stamps and to call on Elizabeth ... We will walk round the fields and look for little creatures in the hedge-backs." So it went on—sometimes quite enjoyable and fun, but it could become tedious when the escort had made other plans. Somehow there was no saying her nay. She commanded a kind of awe and respect coming from such a grand home in such a big city!

She stayed for three weeks and tried in that time to introduce city manners and nursery routine into Anna's life, having unsuccessfully tried it in turn with the older children.

Once again she met with little success, for though Anna liked to hear of Master Reggie's, Miss Winifred's and Miss Irene's doings she had no fancy for aping them. Aunt May's saving grace was that she always brought nice presents, usually including some of her charges' expensive discarded toys and many attractive books. Once she brought a marvellous 'magic lantern' and boxes of fascinating glass slides which was a prized possession for many years. Some outgrown but not outworn stylish clothes of Miss Irene's found their way into Anna's wardrobe and gave her a lot of pleasure.

In return, when she went home she always had a box filled with good things—a pound of freshly made butter, a jar of crab-apple jelly, some rashers of home-fed ham, and an armful of wild flowers, grasses and sprays of leaves which, alas, were wilting even before she got on the train.

Other family visitors were mainly on day visits or short stay, but there was seldom a week in the summer when someone claiming relationship did not avail themselves of a day at the farm, and the larder had to be kept well filled against such contingencies; and if no one turned up, somehow everything was eaten up and the big baking days came round with regular custom.

CHAPTER TWELVE

A COUNTRY SLUM

Anna's pleasant life on the farm, with or without visitors, was a world apart from that of many of her schoolmates—the children of Rockyburn.

That small, slum-like hamlet had been built for the miners when the local pit was first opened. The houses were arranged on three sides of a square, in the midst of which stood a small, grim, red-brick Methodist chapel. The foundation was of black slag, an economical idea on the part of the mine-owners who had no reason for anything better. The houses, all alike, consisted of one single all-purpose room, with the same earth floor, and known as the kitchen; a tiny pantry, little bigger than a cupboard, but big enough to hold all of the food that its owners could afford; and, above, two small bedrooms. The windows were tiny and made not to open and there was no water laid on. Water had to be carried from two communal taps beside the chapel; sanitation consisted of one nauseous earth-closet between every two houses.

Rats and black beetles shared the accommodation and a few hens and goats were to be seen around their owners' doors. Some families were known to take their goat indoors during the winter, others were housed in ram-shackle sheds. Whippets were numerous and received as much or more care than the children in some homes. They were the chief source of entertainment for these men who gambled their few spare coppers on their favourites at the weekend 'coursing.' They were useful too for catching rabbits and hares, often the only meat tasted in some families.

The Old Pit had closed after only a few years of very moderate output, and several attempts at open-cast mining had also failed, with the result that most of the men were now only casual labourers. Those who had been fortunate and had initiative found work in some of the bigger mines of the district and had moved away. Those left in this derelict spot got seasonal work on the farms—potato-picking, haymaking, harvesting and 'snagging' turnips. Some worked on the roads or quarries, breaking stones for roads. Altogether it was a sad, poverty-stricken place, a human scrap-heap without a single redeeming feature.

Even the burn from which it took its name carried leaked sewage from the nearby sewage plant, and the nature of the earth on which the hamlet was built would not even produce grass, let alone trees, flowers or vegetables, had anyone thought of trying to grow them. A few of the more industrious and thoughtful men had tried to grow vegetables on a fertile strip of land edging the burn, but as their crops were invariably stolen during the night by their needy but idle neighbours they soon gave up, but not without many violent fights and brawls.

It was doubtful whether a single book could have been found in any home, unless it were a family Bible which only appeared after a death. And yet there were children there who were attractive and appealing even in their dingy, seldom washed clothes, with their unkempt hair and general air of neglect. One gypsy-like family had children of most striking beauty. One of the girls, who got away in her early teens and made a good marriage, was sought after by local photographers to pose in advertisements for their businesses!

As Anna walked part of the way to and from school with these children she made friends with some of them whilst she shrank rather fearfully from the wilder, uncouth ones.

Her particular fellow traveller was Minnie, two years her senior, and one of eight—seven girls and a boy. It was a mystery to Anna where they all slept but she was too kind to ask. Minnie was bright-eyed, quick, tiny and sparrow-like. She was always cheery and kind, put-on by her older sisters, a willing nursemaid to the younger ones and an adoring slave of the one little boy. Anna thought she was quite wonderful.

"I do wish we could give Minnie some clothes," said Anna one day to her mother. "Do you know, she has *never* in her whole life had a new dress or coat! She always gets the big girls' things and they're old and ragged when they've finished with them."

"We'll see," said her mother—her almost invariable way of making a promise!

That was the beginning of Minnie's changed status. Anna was growing rapidly, leaving Minnie far behind, so as soon as one of her dresses or coats or even boots began to feel a little tight, or was pronounced 'far too short for a big girl like you' it was handed over to the delighted Minnie. It mattered not a jot to her that the children at school all recognized her 'new' clothes as Anna's outgrown ones—she felt like a princess.

This seemed to change Minnie's whole outlook. Always bright and alert though so badly handicapped by her poor home, she now put in a great effort and actually achieved the great success of 'passing the scholarship.' This meant that she would be able to proceed to the high school at the market town of Oakdale, some five miles distant. But alas! there wasn't a hope of Minnie's taking up this wonderful opportunity, and she stayed at the village school just as long as the law demanded, before going to 'service' as her elder sisters had done.

Another family that Anna made friends with on the road were the O'Briens. These were two little Irish lads whose father had come over from his native Ireland hoping to find work in the pits, but he had come at a bad time and soon found himself out of work. He was a big, strong fellow, good-natured and easy-going and often found work at Greenfield. His wife too sometimes gave a hand at extra busy times, such as plucking the geese and turkeys for the Christmas market. The boys, Micky and Paddy, were clean and well-behaved and had a delightful brogue.

"Me Da's after winning a hondred pounds," they told Anna breathlessly one Monday morning.

"Go on!" laughed Anna, unbelievingly.

"Indade, an' it's true," declared Paddy. "It's in the newspaper he buys on Saturdays."

Apparently their father had tried his skill at a puzzle competition in a weekly paper, the prize being £100. Now the solution appeared and, checking over his entry, O'Brien found he had sent in a correct solution.

There was much genuine rejoicing in Rockyburn, for O'Brien was popular and his friends stood to gain a few free pints of beer when the payout was made.

There was a new baby expected very soon so the happy couple lost no time in going to Thickley and purchasing, on credit, a cot, bedding and clothing for all, to the tune of some twenty pounds.

Then the blow fell! The cheque arrived. It was for three pounds, sixteen shillings and sixpence! There had been twenty-six correct entires and the prize money, postage deducted, had been shared.

Anna cried bitterly when she heard the news, which spread more rapidly than the first.

"It's not fair," she sobbed. "Poor Micky and Paddy! And poor Mrs. O'Brien! What will they do with all their nice new things that they can't pay for now?"

What indeed? That was the question everyone was asking. Fortunately the shopkeepers were willing to take back most of the clothes which had not been worn. This left the little boys with a new suit apiece for theirs had soon been pressed into service. These were to be paid for by instalments.

The children of Rockyburn were a thorn in the flesh of Mr. Black for most of them were ineducable, having neither the wish nor the wherewithal to learn. Whether this state of affairs or their shockingly high rate of absenteeism was the worse evil he never could decide. He caned them almost equally on both counts.

The poor clothing, especially the footware, of the children kept them away in bad weather. Those who were sent out in all weathers caught coughs and colds and all the other ailments of childhood, and passed them round the rest. On a wet or snowy day it was no uncommon sight to see some of the Rockyburn children coming to school with a sack folded hood wise over their heads and shoulders as their only approach to an overcoat.

Other reasons for absence, given just as freely by the village children, were domestic ones. Mothers of large broods often kept one of the older girls at home 'to mind the bairns' whilst she struggled with the washing and baking. Another common excuse given by older girls was 'Me mother was bad-in-bed' which often meant she was having another baby, for all the babies were born at home, attended by the village midwife but not always the doctor. He was called in after the event.

It had to be a very sound excuse to escape the cane when the defaulters returned apprehensively to school. The local attendance officer, known as the kiddie-catcher, had a busy time rounding up the missing ones. Threats of fines meant nothing, for there was no money to pay them, so the problem remained and his job was secure.

But to compensate for these erring ones there were some children who rarely missed attendance, and strangely enough these were invariably the farm children who had the furthest to come.

The Rowley twins, Robert and Charles, had the wonderful record of their whole school life—nine years—without an absence! And they had a two-mile walk from home to school. Day in, day out, whatever the weather, they were there, canvas satchels on their backs containing their mid-day meal. This, almost without variation, consisted of thick bacon or cheese sandwiches, a whole currant teacake apiece, a pint of milk to share. Sometimes they would have apples as well. This was all they had between breakfast around half past seven and tea around five, and a day's work and four miles in between. But they remained remarkably healthy and fit and were good at their lessons. Another record was that they had never been caned.

When the time came for them to leave at the age of fourteen, the education authority recognized their achievement by presenting them jointly with a framed certificate, cashing in on the fact that they were twins. There was a so-called public presentation, a very junior clerk from the county office being sent to make it. The boys' parents and one of the school managers were present. The whole ceremony took ten minutes.

Mr. Black, the rest of the staff, and the vicar, were disgusted at the niggardliness of the affair, and out of their own pockets provided each boy with a watch and chain. The vicar also had these engraved, for not only did the boys attend school regularly, they were also in the church choir and seldom missed at least one service each Sunday.

For this second presentation Lowridge rose splendidly to the occasion, and arranged a 'social' in the schoolroom. School mates came and a wonderful, free, 'sit down tea' was provided by the villagers and farmers. There was ham, beef and tongue with suitable trimmings and pickles, cakes of all descriptions and gay, sparkling jellies. Afterwards there were games: trencher, forfeits, postman's knock, and a waltz, polka and a set of lancers for those who likes to dance. Elsie's father and Betty Butterfield were in great demand as pianists.

"It's a good job all of us dusen't come t'school reg'lar," said the school wit, "For t'Master'd be bankrupt buyin' watches, and us would be off school wi' eatin' so much."

No fear of the former contingency arising. The percentage of attendance usually drew the attention of the education authority because it was about the lowest in the county.

CHAPTER THIRTEEN

SCHOOL LEAVERS

At the end of every term there were some leavers who had reached the age of fourteen and were considered to have sufficient education to equip them for the great adventure of life. Few left in a blaze of glory as did the Rowley twins. The most they could expect was a 'reference' if they asked for it, a handshake and a few words of encouragement from the Master. There was a good deal of boasting and bravado by the leavers, who almost all professed themselves to be glad and treated those left behind with mock contempt.

"I'll think of you gettin' two of the best from t'Master when I'm drawin' me pay," boasted Joe Barnes with a wide grin. It was a pitiful jest, however, for poor Joe would be slaving on his father's starve-acre smallholding for his keep alone, for a number of years, and many times would he think wistfully of the fun he'd had with his schoolmates, and the golden leisurely afternoon when they'd watched the 'cubses.'

Sarah Hill, Freda Jones and Emma Green were three friends who had gone through school together. They were glad that they were all leaving together too. They were excited because they had all secured jobs in Oakdale thanks to the good references which Mr. Black had truthfully been able to write for them, for they were all steady, reliable girls who had made the best of their schooldays.

At the end of the summer term they would be leaving school behind; Sarah to serve in a café, Freda to learn millinery and Emma to be an assistant in a large draper's shop, which she referred to grandly as an emporium.

"Fancy us in a town every day!"

"Lovely, isn't it? Better than sticking in Lowridge or Thickley for ever."

"Going in the train every day as well!"

"I'll be getting four-and-six a week—*and* tips, *and* free dinner, and stale cakes to bring home," gloated Sarah, adding quickly, "The cakes are really fresh but if they're broken up you can't serve them to customers."

"I'll only get four shillings and I have to take my own dinner, but of course I'm getting training," volunteered Freda proudly. "An' when I'm trained I might get about twelve shillings a week an' even start a shop of me own," she added dreamily, thinking of all the glamorous hats she would create and adorn with gorgeous ribbon and feathers and gauzy veils.

Emmie was more reticent about her wages, which were pitifully small, but she was terribly proud of the smart outfit the shop would provide—free!

All the assistants wore dark green poplin dresses with white collars and cuffs and belts. "Ooh! They're that stylish! And we can buy a dress-length and a coat at cost price when we've worked there six months," she rolled off happily.

Little did she realize that the cost of the smart outfit came out of her wages which were kept to a meagre four shillings a week till the debt was cleared. Then she would be led to believe that she was getting a generous rise of an extra two shillings.

The three friends were gaily and excitedly facing a prospect of long, tiring days—days that began and ended with a mile walk to and from Thickley station, and quarter of an hour's train journey. The walk would often be taken in dreadful weather and in the dark; the train journey that seemed so grand and sophisticated would eat into their precious, hard-earned wages, a steady and relentless nibble of a few pence a day. They would be at everyone's beck and call and Sarah and Emma would be on their feet most of the day.

But they were young and fearless and ready for anything. Life seemed good. They were the envy of the girls who were going into 'service,' which usually meant as a general servant on some local farm, for there were few private houses around that required maids.

There, on the farms, they would work long hours, doing any rough household tasks, helping with the milking and feeding calves and poultry. They would have plenty of plain food, an icy cold or unbearably stuffy bedroom, small and sparsely furnished. They would have small wages and half a day off once a week. If the farm was a longish distance from their home they would perhaps be given a whole day once a fortnight so they could pay visit home; that is if there was any means of getting there and back. In the evenings they would be found mending or darning to do, or if they went to the village they would have to be back by half past nine at the latest. Eventually they might end up by marrying the farm boy or one of the boys from the village. The more venturesome might answer an advertisement for a servant on a more distant farm, but the life-style would be much the same.

Some of the boys would go to 'farm-place,' where they would fare much the same as the girls. Their work would be rough and heavy; they would learn to handle the big, strong horses, and all the difficult skills of farming, and grow strong on plenty of good, plain food. They might get a weekend visit to their home once in three or four months, but nothing else in the nature of a holiday. In time some would become farm hands with a tied cottage, and the fortunate few might eventually rent a farm of their own.

But when Willie Smart's eldest sister, Margaret, reached leaving age at the end of one Easter term, Willie, two other sisters and two brothers left as well! There was one Smart in each class of the school and two under school age. For they were off to Australia! They were a grand family—nice-looking, healthy and intelligent and touchingly devoted to one another, and though poor they were always neat, clean and well-mannered. Their father, a builder, had decided to accept a government offer to assist emigrants to the Colonies, feeling this would give their large family a chance in life that England did not seem to promise. The parents were right, and though neither of them lived to see the day when Willie was made mayor of a large town they had the satisfaction of seeing them all set on the way to respected, useful and prosperous careers. One boy was to become a doctor, one a partner in a large provision store, two eventually owned a sheep station and the girls married well after interesting careers.

But the little party, with a modest assortment of tin trunks, packing cases and cardboard boxes, waiting on the platform of Thickley station for the train that was to take them on the first stage of this great adventure, was pathetic enough.

Anna and Elsie, with their families, teachers and many of the villagers, were there to see them off. Someone, most likely Mr. Black, started them off singing 'God be with you till we meet again,' and it was a tearful Anna who waved farewell to the gallant boy-friend who had always helped her to get her sums right. Nor was she the only tearful one, for the Smarts in each class had their special affectionate friends, and school and village were the poorer for their going.

CHAPTER FOURTEEN

PRIZES AND HOLIDAYS

The summer holidays were always greeted with joyous relief by the teachers and children alike. The latter had been through a fortnight's strain on their mental powers, doing exams, the results of which decided whether they would 'go up' or 'stop down.' Those in the latter category, in Mr. Black's time, almost all received some punishment in addition to their disgrace, for he seemed under the impression that ignorance was part of the original sin and had to be beaten out.

The four children, two boys and two girls, who came top and second in each class, on the other hand, were handsomely rewarded for their achievement. As Anna and Elsie vied for the top girl's position and occupied it alternately almost all year round, the tension became a strain even on their close friendship as prize-day drew near.

Mr. Black and the vicar generously added to the small allowance allocated for prizes by the educational authority.

"It's the only way most of them will possess a book," sighed the Master when a friend expressed the opinion that he was over-generous on his small salary.

He was right, too, and the books were greatly treasured and read over and over again. 'Alice in Wonderland,' 'The Water Babies,' 'Black Beauty,' 'Little Women,' 'Ivanhoe' and many another classic found their way into homes where even the parents read them, and proudly showed them to admiring or envious relations.

"If I get a prize this time it'll be my third," said Anna, trying not to sound too hopeful.

"You will," returned Elsie, a trifle snappily. They had counted up their marks and Anna was leading by four, but alas! she had some blots and crossing-out on her composition paper, while her rival's work was literally spotless, so there was still a teasing uncertainty, for with Mr. Black neatness most certainly counted. In fact the vicar agreed that some of *his* prizes should be for neatness alone.

The breaking up day arrived and all the school assembled in the big room for the prize giving. Wonderful piles of books of all sizes, and with lovely bright covers, were on view on a table at the front. The children were flushed and bright-eyed with excitement. Even the poor little unlucky ones who hadn't a hope of winning one gazed with wistful admiration at the display.

The vicar had been asked to present them and was ready and waiting. The Master made a few remarks about the results in general, mainly for the vicar's benefit, for the children had already heard and *felt* his judgement. Then the lucky ones were named, starting with the little ones of Standard 1.

What pride and trembling delight was revealed on those little faces as the vicar placed the precious gift in eager little hands! Their mouths were dry with emotion and their 'Thank you, Sir' came out in a squeak or a whisper.

Their schoolmates and brothers and sisters beamed with a pride rarely shown and gave each a hearty clap.

Elsie and Anna did not look at one another. They were both very pale and trembling a little, and the slightest thing could have sent them into hysterical giggles or tears.

"And now we come to Standard 4," announced the vicar when they felt they couldn't stand it a moment longer.

"The girls' first prize is a double one, for two girls have done such excellent work we felt we could not call them first and second. Anna Crosby and Elsie Dent have each been deemed worthy of the prize. Anna leads by four marks but Elsie makes up by neatness. Come forward, girls."

Anna's prize was a lovely copy of 'Black Beauty' while Elsie received 'Christy's Old Organ,' books they were to read and re-read, and always with tears!

The second prize now went to a surprised and delighted Jenny, who had never had such luck before.

At last the ceremony was over, many starry-eyed youngsters happily clutching their rewards. The next year's classes were read out, a few words of advice given to the leavers, a hymn and a prayer and then—Hurrah for a whole month's holiday!

Summer holidays! A week at the seaside; family picnics; visits to beauty spots and places of historic interest?

For the children of Lowridge C. of E. school such delights were as unknown or as unlikely as a visit to the moon! Indeed it was hardly likely that the teachers would aspire to such treats. Certainly Miss Manley and Betty, on their unpaid holiday, would not be able to go far afield.

Half a dozen or so of the children, Anna among them, would go to stay a few days with grandparents or aunts in surroundings and circumstances not greatly different from their own.

Anna and fifteen-year-old Hugh would go to their uncle's farm some twelve miles away, and would find it excitingly different because there was a real river bounding their uncle's fields. Their cousins had dammed it at one spot so they would have the unusual delight of bathing, and there was fishing too. They would also be taken to a picture house in the nearby small town and be thrilled with a cowboy film.

Then the two boy cousins would return to Greenfield with them and they would be just as delighted with the exchange.

"It's a lovely holiday," Anna told Elsie after her last year's visit. "But I *did* get homesick and I was pleased when I'd got it over."

For there was everything one could wish for at Greenfield —lovely trees to climb or just to sit under and play with the latest kittens; a shallow, pebbly little beck over-arched with bushes and trees—perfect for playing at jungle or story-book adventures. There was the swing hung from the great ash tree where one could perform wonderful acrobatic feats or just swing and dream; bramble hedges, where towards the end of the holiday one could soon fill a basket with luscious berries; early mornings with dewy pastures when one had the never-failing thrill of finding exquisite, satin-topped, pink-lined mushrooms. There was the fun of harvest teas in the sunny, stubbly fields and rides in the empty harvest carts returning to the field for more loads.

All these and a hundred other simple delights, whether shared with Elsie, the visiting cousins or aunt, with her brothers and sisters, or just as contentedly on her own, made Anna's home the best place in the world for a summer holiday. A day trip to the seaside with the Sunday School, and a day's shopping with tea in a café at Oakdale with her mother, completed the holiday bliss.

Elsie, however, thought herself vastly superior to her schoolmates in the matter of holidays. She was going to stay again, as she had done ever since she was six, with really *rich* people in a grand big house in Newcastle—as remote from Lowridge as London.

Her mother and aunt, both good dressmakers, had been busy for some time making her some new clothes for the visit, and the coat that had been new for Whit Sunday had to be sponged and pressed "It takes two hours by train," she told Anna proudly, not mentioning the long wait for a connection at Oakdale. But this Anna knew all about because of Aunt May's travelling tribulations.

An admiring and envious group of listeners gathered round in the playtime one day just before school broke up. Elsie was regaling them with tales of her previous visits to the big city.

"I call her Auntie, but she's really my godmother," she explained. "She used to stay at the hall when my mother was a maid there and she liked Mum so very much so she said she would be my godmother …"

The little crowd listening to the romantic tale included Freda and Sarah, who did not usually condescend to this extent to a youngster so much lower in school.

"Tell us about the house," begged Freda, dreaming of the day when having made her fortune as a high-class milliner she too would live in a grand house.

"Well," Elsie drew a big breath. "It's got a drawing room, a dining room, and a study and a proper bathroom with gold taps and a lav in, an' it's got five bedrooms and some attics, an' it's got bee-utiful carpets all over." She paused to get her breath.

"Hasn't it got a kitchen or a pantry?" asked the practical Minnie, whose small domestic world was bounded by those two domains.

"Oh, of course!" said Elsie with a toss of her curls. "But Auntie doesn't like me to go in there much, in case I get in the way of the cook and the maid."

"By! Have they got servants?" incredulously, from Sarah.

"Of course!"

"What do you *do* there?" someone asked.

"Well, Auntie takes me to the lovely big shops and sometimes we have tea in a res'trant. It's smart! All the tables have flowers on in silver vases, an' there's a band playing on a stage all set with palm trees. There's men waiters as well as ladies."

Sarah's eyes popped, ambition stirring.

"What else?"

"She takes me to visit her friends that have children and I play in their nursery. They have a doll's house that the little girl can get into and a rocking horse an' a magic lantern…"

Seeing that the older girls were losing interest, Elsie produced her choicest titbit.

"They call their mother 'Mamma-dear'."

Squeals of derision greeted this announcement and even Elsie joined in the giggling, and the group broke up.

Yes, indeed, this was the great opportunity for Elsie to put into practice the ladylike manners her mother had been at such pains to instil. She must have given complete satisfaction to her hostess for each year she returned home generously endowed with a new winter overcoat, and several second-hand but excellent clothes from the nursery-world.

Once the two friends had 'got over' their away visits they had a two-way visit system for the rest of the holiday. At Elsie's they played in the back yard where the wash-house made a splendid place to play at mothers-and-fathers, acting out Elsie's grand experiences and bringing up with the utmost refinement and gentility pretend children with high-class names of Cecil, Hubert and Geraldine; indeed they would often refer to it as 'playing Cecil.' When they tired of these delectable games they showed off their piano-playing, or joined the other village children in wildly exhilarating games of hide and seek and chasing all around the village.

Elsie's return visits were equally happily spent. The setting for mothers-and-fathers was now a grass-grown stone quarry, whose graded slopes and shelving ledges lent themselves well to becoming a spacious and gracious mansion. Hide and seek, sometimes joined in by the servant girl on her afternoon off, now involved diving under piles of soft, sweet-smelling hay, or climbing into lofts and mangers. The days flew by with incredible speed, and a new school year was upon them.

CHAPTER FIFTEEN

WAR BRINGS CHANGES

The year the girls moved up into the Master's class began under shadow for just a fortnight previously war had been declared. It was August 1914. Even the children's faces were sober and anxious as they assembled on the triangle that first morning, for war was the one topic of conversation, and wild rumours and conjectures were afloat.

"Me Da says all the men and lads will ha' t' go," one small boy announced knowingly.

"By! I 'ope our Da has to!" gloated Jimmy Sprott, whose constant brutal 'beltings' from his drunken father were not a cause for respect or affection.

Mr. Black addressed the morning assembly with extra solemnity, urging the children to work hard 'for England's sake' and for once there were no threats appended.

In spite of the clouds of war, Anna was thrilled to be in Standard 5. She was the youngest in the class, being Elsie's junior by three weeks, and was eager to acquit herself well, and for knowledge. In spite, too, of the Master's outbursts of temper which she dreaded, she knew, as did all the brighter children, that he was a good teacher and his lessons were full of interest.

As usual, she and Elsie were sitting together in the 'top' seats, but the year they greatly missed Willie Smart and did not much care for Harry Arnold who had taken his place. Harry, unlike the generous Willie, was more inclined to copy their correct answers than to help them, and to gloat when they made mistakes. However under Mr. Black's eagle eye there would be little opportunity for either case.

Soon the men and youths of the district began to go to the war in increasing numbers. One child after another announced with sadness, pride or relief, according to the nature of the relationship, the departure of yet another potential soldier.

"Me Uncle Chris an' me Uncle Bob's gone."

"Our John's away."

"Our Da's gone."

Mostly it was pride that triumphed, for the appeal to patriotism and duty was heard on every side, and posters, newspapers and hoardings, as well as recruiting meetings, all proclaimed:

"YOUR KING AND YOUR COUNTRY NEED YOU!"

Even the most insignificant, the idlers, the out-of-work and the casual labourers, who for so long had never counted for anything, came into their own, and the transformation in many of them was unbelievable. At last their children had something to boast about.

"My Da'll be a gen'ral soon," prophesied Billy Foster. "He's got a stripe already."

"You mean a corp'ral," corrected Clive Green, scornfully.

"Oh well, maybe—it's something like that anyway," conceded Billy, in no way dampened.

Alas! Billy's father was killed even before he got his second stripe.

Anna's eldest brother, who was married and lived in another county, had enlisted at once; Elizabeth's husband had gone; Philip, who had been in the Officers' Training Corps at college, now got a commission as he relinquished his first teaching post. Steve, eager and straining to be off like his brothers, was desperately disappointed because a committee known as the Farmers' Tribunal had decided that he must remain on the farm to carry on its more-than-ever vital work. As the sources of casual labour steadily declined, Steve worked as hard and as loyally, if not as dangerously, as any soldier. Hugh, now nearly seventeen, was secretly hoping the war would last long enough for him to get into it, at eighteen. Anna was terribly proud of them all—and of her sisters too, who were now land girls—and wore trousers!—and did men's work. They were also engaged to soldiers.

Elsie's father, being rather lame and working at munitions, was exempt from the army, but she had two cousins to boast about, and her godmother's husband was actually a *Major*.

The war had certainly made its inroads into families in village, hamlet and farm. In school, too, it edged in. Paper became scarce, and the detested slates abandoned so joyfully only a year ago, were produced again. New books of any description were out of the question so the children read and re-read all the old ones till they knew them off by heart.

Songs took on a martial note:

'We can depend on Young Australi-ar,
On Indi-ar
And Canad-ar too …
For they have proved themselves in Afric-ar
A patriotic pattern to the world!'

the children patriotically proclaimed; and in similar mood they enjoyed 'Tipperary' and 'Pack up your troubles in your old kit bag.' The hymns took up the theme:

'Land of our birth, we pledge to thee …'

And as they sang, 'Holy Father in Thy mercy, Hear our anxious prayer …' many of the older girls would weep unrestrainedly.

The boys as well as the girls took up knitting as the winter campaigns approached, and the endless skeins of khaki wool were wound into great balls which in turn were knitted into seemingly endless mufflers, gloves and balaclavas.

"Could we have a knitting club?" suggested Mary Hilton, the top girl in the school. "We could give up our playtimes and stay back an hour at night." Her suggestion was approved and under the guidance of the women teachers the busy little knitters turned out an amazing amount of 'comforts for our brave men.'

As the war entered into its second year, with Anna and Elsie now in Standard 6, the greatest change at school was to take place. Mr. Black announced that he was leaving. He was turned forty and had not been called up, so his volunteering was much admired. The fact that he would never see 'active service' in its direct form but would be employed in a clerical position in England did not detract from his glory, and the school gave him a rousing send-off, old scores wiped out. The knitting club provided him with a complete set of 'comforts' and Mary Hilton, coached by Miss Stewart, made a moving little speech.

Miss Manley had already left for the W.A.A.C., and a new regime had started in the infants. Mrs. Gould, a middle-aged widow who had left teaching many years ago, returned to take charge there. The former gaiety and laughter was sadly missing, though there was no lack of kindness and care.

Betty Butterfield had renounced her intention of going to college as women teachers were so badly needed to fill the gaps left by the men going a-soldiering. The fact that she and Steve were now openly 'courting' helped them to bear their double disappointment—his at being debarred from the army and hers at missing much-looked-forward-to college.

She stayed on, and now being given that status of 'uncertified assistant' had to be addressed as *Miss* Butterfield. She was a very capable and 'born teacher' and was to prove a valuable asset to the school and village. Standards 1 and 2 became her little world, in addition to which she continued to be the school's accompanist and succeeded Mr. Black as church organist. Miss Stewart, also now a very efficient and confident teacher, became 'acting head' for a brief spell.

"Wonder if we'll get a real head?" was the general theme among the children.

"Likely another woman," said some boys in disgust, and everyone groaned in sympathy.

But they were wrong. One day Mr. Allwood arrived. Pale, thin and wearing very thick glasses and obviously very nervous, he was fighting a losing battle from the start. After the stern and often harsh discipline of Mr. Black and the no-nonsense approach of Miss Stewart, his plaintive nagging and half-hearted exhortations were completely ignored by the rough element, of whom there was now a large proportion. Now that many fathers were away from home many of the older children had become wilder and more openly defiant. Even the normally well-behaved ones could not resist taking advantage of the new man's weakness, and the work, behaviour and even attendance rapidly deteriorated. Now to have a few days off meant a feeble reproach, not a dreaded caning as in Mr. Black's day.

The climax was reached in his second term. Though normally 'soft' on mis-doers he was, on occasion, violent with the cane and, unlike Mr. Black, gave girls as heavy punishment as boys.

Maggie Burns, in Standard 5, had done some careless, untidy work, wasting—as he pointed out—the precious ration of paper that came their way. She was a simple, thin, little creature, timid and under-fed, and as she stood trembling, waiting for the cane, a little pool appeared at her feet. John, her big brother in Standard 7, strode to her side and put his arm round her protectively, facing Mr. Allwood defiantly. The teacher shouldered him roughly aside.

"Hold out your hand," he shouted at Maggie, as he raised the cane.

Quick as lightening John snatched it, broke it across his knee and threw the two pieces in the air. In doing so he accidentally knocked off Mr. Allwood's glasses, rendering him practically helpless, for his sight was very poor.

"You'll not use that again!" yelled John and the excited class cheered and stamped their feet.

Hearing the uproar, Miss Stewart came in, and taking in the situation at a glance, she ordered John out of the room and quelled the others. This gave Mr. Allwood the opportunity of recovering his glasses and at least a little of his composure.

Acting on Miss Stewart's orders John apologized in front of the whole school, for of course the story spread like wildfire. Later, Mr. Allwood was big enough to make a little speech in front of his own classes, commending John for defending his sister and shaking him by the hand!

This incident, so surprising to all concerned, slightly raised the children's opinion of Mr. Allwood, and for a while the behaviour improved. Nevertheless he left at the end of his second term.

Once again the guessing and surmising began about the future head of the school, but they had to wait until they assembled after Easter holiday to have their answer.

CHAPTER SIXTEEN

A NEW ORDER

"It doesn't look as if there's a new boss; there's only old Scotch Broth," remarked Harry Arnold as they stood around on the triangle on the first morning of the new term. The bell stopped and Miss Stewart came to the door to get them in. She had now become very much a part of the school and had an air of natural dignity and authority which commanded respect. Though she very rarely condescended to using the cane she had her own efficient methods of dealing with defaulters and it seemed not at all unlikely that she should be in command once more.

The children were greatly surprised, when, on entering the big room, to see a tall, handsome young man at the Master's desk. At best they might have expected someone obviously physically unfit for war service, or someone too old. But there he was—broad-shouldered, very erect, with crisp brown curly hair, tanned face and twinkling blue eyes—a very picture of fitness!

Miss Stewart put an end to their gaping incredulity by saying brightly, "Now children, this is your new Master, Mr. Luke, say 'Good morning sir',"

"Good morning, sir," they chorused.

"Good morning, children," returned the smiling Mr. Luke. Hymns and prayers over, Mr. Luke spoke quietly to the children, who had all paid keen attention. He told them that he had heard lots about them, and although some of those things were not entirely in their favour, such as poor attendance, he was sure they weren't such a bad lot. He went on a little while in semi-bantering style, and a few times, uncertain grins appeared here and there, and some rather scornful smirks from the oldest boys who were beginning to think him 'a bit soft.' But he soon corrected that mistake. Friendly, fair and reasonably patient, he gave them to understand, but he expected from them only the *best* that they were capable of, and intended to get it. The grins and smirks faded out.

The puzzlement of the children over his exemption from the war, when he looked so young and healthy, was soon solved. The explanation soon got round—Miss Stewart saw to that, for though she was engaged and finally happily married to a handsome, kilt-swinging Scot from a fine and famous regiment, she greatly liked and admired the new head. She had no intention of letting the children or their parents think him a shirker, as they were now inclined to label indiscriminately any fit young man not in uniform. The truth was that Mr. Luke's unusually erect and somewhat rigid bearing was due to the fact that he wore a steel brace to support his spine and he also had a steel plate in one leg. One of the first volunteers, he had soon been in action and had received many serious wounds. He had been in hospital for a long time and finally was discharged and allowed to take up again his interrupted vocation.

And a vocation it was. He really loved teaching and he loved and understood children—the ideal combination for the job.

Anna, like all the girls and most of the boys, fell under his spell. Work and even attendance improved all round and a happy atmosphere was felt. The mildest rebuke, rare as it was, could bring tears to Anna's eyes. Elsie, though not so sensitive, thought he was wonderful and went out of her way to win his favour. A spirit of rivalry for his attention grew between the two friends, sometimes sadly testing their long-standing friendship.

The schoolhouse, vacated by Mr. Black and his wife, had stood empty since then, as Mr. Atwood being unmarried had been in lodgings. Now Mr. Luke, whose furniture had arrived on his first day, lived there alone and had engaged one of the village women to cook and clean for him daily.

"My mother's going to ask Mr. Luke to dinner on Sunday." Elsie dropped this bomb one Friday as school ended.

"Oh!" Anna gasped, stricken with envy. Why, oh why hadn't her family thought of this first? She turned away at a loss for words.

Elsie relented. "Why don't you come a bit earlier for Sunday School and call for me? He'll still be there."

"Oh! Could I?" Anna brightened. "I'll do that."

Though it was raining cats and dogs on Sunday afternoon Anna, to her mother's surprise, did not try to make this an excuse, reasonable enough for once, to stay at home. Instead she took an umbrella, without her usual protest against it, and set off across the wet fields a good half hour before she needed to.

Her hardihood was rewarded, for, looking very much at ease, there was Mr. Luke, chatting to Elsie's parents. Anna was welcomed in, her wet coat put to dry and she joined the little group by the fire.

"Come on, Anna. Sit by me," said her hero, making room for her on the sofa. She accepted the invitation, blushing and tongue-tied with shyness.

Elsie's mother had proudly told Mr. Luke about her daughter's good voice and now she was going to sing for him. Her father sat down at the piano and Elsie sang with great sweetness 'Rose-bud in the heather.' It really was delightful and Mr. Luke was genuinely charmed. Anna felt forlorn and downcast, much as she admired her friend's gift.

"And what can my other sweetheart do?" asked that understanding young man, giving Anna an encouraging smile.

"She can play the piano!" said Elsie, quick and generous.

"Indeed!" he feigned surprise. "Well, come on then. Let me hear you."

Anna, scarlet and nervous, sat down at the piano. She would do her *very* best ... She thought of her favourite piece, 'The Harmonious Blacksmith,' and with a firm touch, and remembering all the 'expression' her teacher had taught her, she played it without a mistake.

"Beautiful!" exclaimed Mr. Luke. "Two gifted young ladies in so small a village school!" He did not sound as if he were teasing at all. They went to Sunday School the best of friends, each equally sure of his favour.

That was one of the new master's gifts—he could make any child feel loved and important and yet not cause any feelings of jealousy or favouritism. Warm-hearted and full of real Christian charity, he wanted everyone to enjoy life as he did. He realized that to be happy a child had to feel needed. Insecure, ignorant and almost uneductable children, accustomed to being ignored, ridiculed and even punished for their shortcomings, blossomed out under him as they had not done since they left Miss Manley's understanding care.

For Mr. Luke soon revealed that each one had *something* that he or she could do well.

Alice Farley, adenoidal and slow, unable to read at thirteen years of age, was discovered to have a flair for 'tidying up,' so he put her in charge of the big cupboard where the classes' books were kept in a chaotic state of disorder. They were dog-eared, had pages falling out and broken bindings. Alice re-arranged the whole contents of the cupboard neatly and methodically, and spent lots of time with paste and brush patching up the worst of the books. And in her quiet and simple way she saw to it that the new orderliness was maintained. She heard herself being praised for the first time in the big school!

Norman Binks, who couldn't get the simplest sum right at the first attempt, and who stammered so painfully that it was impossible to tell whether he could read or not, had made a most unhappy progress up the school. Mr. Luke, finding that he was good with his hands, taught him lettering, and he did this so beautifully that after a short while the vicar asked him to print a bill about the harvest festival. When it was displayed in the village shop window, Norman's pride knew no bounds, especially as Mr. Luke had added clearly in one corner: 'Printing by Norman Binks, age 11.'

He received several requests to print notices after this, and so greatly was his confidence established that his stammering gradually ceased and it was found that he could read after all!

Next began a campaign of personal hygiene and generally improving the appearance. Anna, Elsie and a sprinkling of girls throughout the school always had neat and attractive, if plain, clothes and took trouble to polish their boots from time to time. These fortunate ones Mr. Luke held up as an example to the rest. On a Monday morning he would have them out in front of the school, and as they blushed and wriggled uncomfortably he would point out their various attractions. It seemed hard on the little ragamuffins from Rockyburn and other poverty-line homes, but with his gift for tact and kindness Mr. Luke managed to install a little personal pride in them. New hair ribbons, a tablet of scented soap, a comb, a tin of boot polish would find their way unobtrusively into the pockets of the most needy, and the results, in some cases at least, far outlasted the gifts.

The war news was sombre and depressing, bringing anxiety and sorrow to many homes, but the new Master, with the full support of his staff, was determined to keep its shadows as far from the children as possible, and school became a little oasis where each day there was some lightness of heart, and relief from the prevailing grimness around.

CHAPTER SEVENTEEN

ENTER MRS. LUKE

The news had soon spread that Mr. Luke was married, but that his wife was nursing her ailing mother. Now, the latter having recovered, Mrs. Luke was coming to join her husband.

"We'll not have so much fun with him now," the children prophesied sadly. At weekends he had taken to to having a game of cricket with the boys on the green; taking a little crowd of them for a long walk or picnic; or on one memorable half-holiday giving them a thrilling cross-country paper-chase. His physical handicap was sometimes very noticeable but he never referred to it and even the toughest and roughest boys felt, perhaps for the first time, the stirrings of consideration and sympathy.

Mrs. Luke, young, pretty and smiling, arrived at last and came across to assembly the very next morning. The staff and children were introduced to her. She told them she was so pleased with the way they had welcomed her and looked after her husband in her absence that she wanted them all to come for tea! However, as their home was not big enough, they'd have to hold the tea-party in the school on Saturday.

This was exciting! The children began to clap. The coming of the Master's wife wasn't going to spoil things after all.

Saturday morning found the teachers, half a dozen of the oldest girls and Mrs. Luke busily making sandwiches, setting the tables and generally creating a very festive setting for the party.

The children arrived at two o' clock. Never, except on the day of the scripture examination, had there been such an effort at smartness! The girls wore their very best dresses and the boys had been liberal with the 'tap-oil.' The tablets of soap, combs and boot polish had been put to good use, and faces and shoes vied in shining.

A programme of games, races and skipping contests had been arranged and these took place on the green with a crowd of spectators urging their children on with good-humoured banter and chaff. There were prizes too—packets of sweets, now scarce and dear.

Then they all went in to tea. Eyes grew big and faces beamed as the children saw the wonderful spread and took their places at the trestle tables. They sang the grace which they sang daily before dismissing for dinner, but today it meant so much more:

'Be present at our table, Lord,
Be here and everywhere adored;
Thy creatures bless and grant that we
May feast in Paradise with thee.'

Well a feast it certainly was, and there was no doubt that it was a little Paradise for many of these children who had so few treats.

Mrs. Luke was considered a worthy partner for the Master, and like him she showed a practical interest in the children. A good needlewoman, she invited any of the oldest girls who wished to a sewing class at her house, teaching them to use her sewing machine, and many of them had the thrill of making their own dresses; and some from the poorest homes learned many niceties of home craft that they had no other means of learning. The Luke's home was not luxurious in any way, but was simply furnished in good taste, and the youngsters thought it was wonderful.

"We've never made nice things at school," one of the girls told her. "We always start off learning stitches on the little bits of calico—we call them specimens. First we learned to hem and then we made a duster; then it was run-and-fell and we had to make a pillowcase; then it was gathers so we made an apron. I hated sewing till you came, and now I love it." A compliment indeed.

The khaki knitting, never-ending it seemed, had begun to pall a little even on those most willing to 'do their bit.' So Mr. Luke decided he would direct their efforts in another area, and to another good cause, of which there was an abundance.

They would have a *concert*, to raise money for the Red Cross. He announced this one morning after prayers, and there was little work done that morning. Excitement and surmise ran at fever-heat.

"I hope we do a sketch."

"Ooh yes! A funny one with dressin' up an' that."

"I saw one once at Thickley. There was this man ..."

"Oh shut up! Mr. Luke'll know some better ones than Thickley folks does."

"Elsie you'll have to sing."

"Well, I might."

"You can play the pianner-Anna." (an oft-repeated witticism).

"There'll be no concert of you don't get on with your work." The threat was not serious as they well knew, but it had the desired effect and heads were bent over arithmetic problems for a while.

Rehearsals were soon going at top speed. Yes! There was to be a sketch and hearts beat faster as parts were cast. Four boys and six girls were needed and they could just manage them out of Standard 7. No-one but the teachers knew that Mr. Luke had added a character to make this just right. It was a part involving only two 'yes-es' and a 'no' but it was enough for the painfully shy Esther, who had an impediment yet longed desperately to be in it.

Action songs, recitations, solos, piano solos, a sword dance and a fairy dance completed the programme. Everyone had a chance to be in something, and everyone had the chance, so longed for, to dress up, if it was only to wear a policeman's helmet, or a shawl and apron to be a granny!

Drawers and cupboards were ransacked, yards of sixpence-a-yard butter muslin dyed, lace curtains temporarily borrowed and sheep's wool collected for wigs and beards.

Mrs. Gould and Miss Butterfield trained the smallest children, while the Master and Miss Stewart worked with the rest, often helped by Mrs. Luke. A number of parents readily gave their assistance with the costumes, the village joiner erected a platform in the 'raised' room and provided simple screens and props.

And now Norman Binks' talent was put to good use. Provided with red, white and blue chalks and large sheets of paper he made some splendid bills lavishly decorated with Union Jacks and other patriotic emblems. These were displayed in several village windows just to make sure that no-one was left unaware of the spectacular treat awaiting them. Even Rockyburn had its own bill pasted on the chapel wall. The vicar, full of enthusiasm, caused an atmosphere of awed excitement when he commissioned three bills to be displayed in Thickley.

"By! Fancy if Thickley folks came down to see us!"

"Why, it'll be as good as owt they can do."

"Ee! Ah'm scared. Ah'll forget me part."

Elsie and Anna were practising diligently at home and, in addition to 'The Merry Peasant,' Anna was going to play a duet with Harry Arnold, 'By the Sad Sea Waves.' She was at great pains to get Harry not to 'thump' but it was an uphill fight, for *he* was at great pains to show that there was nothing effeminate about boy's music!

Harry's *pièce de résistance* was 'The Battle March of Delhi' and even Anna had to admit that his 'thumping' made it sound ever so thrilling.

At last rehearsals were completed and the date fixed. It was autumn, the nights were drawing in and an evening's entertainment was such an unwonted treat for the neighbourhood that the tickets went like hot cakes.

It was a huge success from start to finish. The big room was packed to its limits with all available relatives and friends of the young performers. A sprinkling of khaki-clad Da-s, big brothers and uncles and even one hero in hospital blue added the necessary touch of sentiment to the bill's announcement: All Proceeds in Aid of Our Gallant Men.

Anna's father, who could be counted on for a generous donation, acted as chairman, but to Anna's great relief spoke very briefly.

Action songs by the Infants came first, before the night's excitement had exhausted them. Proud parents gazed in awe at the unsuspected talents of their offspring.

The comedy sketch by the oldest pupils was voted 'as good as anything in theatre' though it was doubtful if the audience had ever been to a theatre. Somehow Esther managed to get her 'yes-es' and 'no-s' reversed but it only added to the hilarity.

The musical items aroused great admiration. Harry excelled with his flourishes and crashes, and it was prophesied solemnly that he would 'go far.'

And so, through the whole programme, all the performers rose splendidly to the occasion, and all were sorry when it was time for 'God Save The King,' but they sang it none the less lustily, standing rigidly at attention in the best military style.

The takings were nine pounds, one shilling, and Anna's father made it up to £10. A great night to remember.

CHAPTER EIGHTEEN

FACTS OF LIFE DISCOVERED

It was quite some time before the excitement and chatter about the concert died down and the children settled down to normal routine. Then the girls noticed that Mrs. Luke was not so much involved in school activities. The biggest disappointment came when she said she was temporarily giving up the sewing club, but that Miss Stewart had kindly promised to continue till all the garments had been finished. The club, now held in the school, was not nearly the attraction it had been in the cosy home of the Lukes, so the first spell of wintry weather was an excuse for it to disband, and the khaki knitting was resumed with dutiful sighs.

"I know why Mrs. Luke gave up the club," Elsie whispered importantly to Anna one morning as they got their heads together over a section of the Catechism that they were supposed to be learning.

"I expect she got tired of us trampling on her nice carpet—that's what my mother says," returned Anna rather snappily. She was peeved that Elsie seemed always one jump ahead of her in matters pertaining to the Luke ménage.

"No, it's not that."

"Well, what then?"

"She's going to get a baby."

"Oh!" Anna was astounded. Then, "Who told you?" she demanded.

"I heard Mother talking to Mrs. Harden about it. Anyway, you can see!"

"Eee! You *are* rude, Elsie!"

They giggled quietly and were recalled to their duty by a mild reproach from Mr. Luke.

When playtime came round they shyly approached Edie Harden, a fourteen-year-old girl just on the verge of leaving. She was the grand-daughter of Mrs. Harden, the village midwife. A nice, sensible and kind girl, Edie had already given

Anna a simple introduction to the facts of life insofar as they related to its continuance.

This had happened one day in spring when Edie had accompanied Anna to the farm. On the way they had seen ewe giving birth to a lamb, and had watched, half fascinated, half embarrassed. Anna had been brought up to regard these farm incidents as something that children should not know anything about. Lambs, calves, foals, kittens and puppies were born with rhythmic regularity, but *how* was not for children to bother about, much less see! She would not have dreamed of asking her mother or even her sisters the how-s or why-s of it all. In any case she would have been told, "You'll get to know when you need to!"

The Rockyburn children, in the cramped living space, had heard and seen most of the mysteries of procreation and birth, and some of their crude and garbled descriptions had come to the ears of Anna from time to time, but she had shamefacedly kept them to herself, or giggled, a little embarrassed, with Elsie about them. Generally however, because of their dislike of the slummy character and the ugly language of the Rockyburn crowd, they dismissed their theories as 'rude talk.' Elsie professed to know 'a lot about it' but when pressed had little but old wives' tales to recount.

Edie had simply told Anna that 'the father plants a seed in the mother and it grows into a baby,' and Anna had been satisfied, so now Edie seemed the most likely person to enlighten them on the vital question.

"Yes, it's true," she told them. "My Gran'ma's going to look after her. It'll be in about two month's time."

"It takes nine months altogether," Elsie exclaimed, proud of her knowledge.

"Mm," Edie nodded.

"I know how to tell if it'll be a girl or a boy," Elsie went on, warming to the subject.

Edie laughed. "No-one can tell," she said.

"Yes," Elsie was certain. "If the mother puts blue ribbons on the dresses and things she going to get a boy and if she puts pink it'll be a girl. My mother had pink ribbons when she got me."

Edie laughed again, but good naturedly, adding, "Well if we wait we'll see."

There was a good deal of whispering and gossiping among the girls—the imminent arrival of the Luke baby brought the forbidden topics to the surface and Anna and Elsie added a number of new facts to their hitherto ignorant notions. They learned to their surprise that a girl could have a baby without being married, but that it was a wicked and sinful thing to happen. This solved the mystery of Joseph Taylor and his mother, Meggie-Ann.

Joseph was a thin, white-faced little boy of about three who had recently come with his mother to live in the village. Meggie-Ann was also thin and white-faced and pathetically young. They were staying with the girl's grandmother, who herself had not long lived there. There was no sign of a father; they were terribly poor and they kept themselves to themselves.

The old woman was unkind to the pair of them and lost no opportunity of loudly voicing her dislike of them. Elsie had frequently heard her calling Joseph a bastard and asked her mother the meaning of the word. With the prevailing idea that children should be kept in ignorance of such things, Elsie's mother said that it meant that little Joseph had no father!

"Well, the poor little thing!" exclaimed Elsie with indignation. "I expect his father got killed in the war so his rotten old granny should be extra good to them."

"That's enough!" admonished her mother. "Anyway it's none of your business ..." and there the matter was closed.

But now they were learning! They began to understand several other hushed-up incidents. There was sixteen-year-old Violet Gibbs, who was sent away when she complained of being sick every day. The two girls had thought her mother was very unkind. They had often asked how Violet was and when she would be coming home, and had received evasive answers. They had been puzzled and indignant of hearing a village woman refer to Violet as 'a downright bad girl,' for Violet had always been so jolly and good-natured and all the boys liked her.

She was away for a year and when she returned she brought a small baby with her. Her mother gave out that it was an orphan relative that they had adopted. Now in the light of their new discoveries Elsie and Anna realized that the 'orphan' was remarkably like Violet with the same snub nose, carroty hair and wide, laughing mouth.

Life was certainly beginning to be complicated, and Anna felt saddened as she was introduced to some of its sordidness. Babies had always seemed such delightful, loveable, heaven-sent little things; now she saw that they could bring sorrow, deceit and unkindness into a home; that it could even be a sin to have one.

The birth of the Luke baby, just before Christmas, was a wonderful uplifting antidote to this sad phase. It was a boy, born during the night. Next morning a beaming Mr. Luke announced the good news at assembly, and the children beamed back at him.

At playtime, he kept Edie, Anna and Elsie back when the rest went out.

"How would you like to see my little son?" he asked them.

"Ooh!" Their gasps of delighted surprise were sufficient answer.

"Come on then!"

Off they went to the schoolhouse, elated yet strangely shy. Mrs. Harden was in charge and opened the door to them. Mr. Luke took them upstairs, and, finger on lip, peeped into the bedroom and then beckoned them in.

"I've brought three eager little friends to see our boy," he told his wife, looking at her adoringly.

"There was a dainty basket-cot hung with frilly muslin curtains and the girls bent over it to gaze at the most perfect, adorable baby imaginable, and the youngest any of them had ever seen. Anna's heart was filled with love and delight—she could not find any words.

Elsie, ever eager to say the right thing, burst out in genuine admiration, "Oh! He's so beautiful, and so like his mother," and Edie murmured agreement.

Their tongues were loosened when they got outside, and they had a happy story to tell the other girls.

"An' did you notice," Elsie said, turning to Edie, "There were blue bows on the cot curtains? That shows I *was* right about them knowing it would be a boy!"

Edie laughed. "Yes, I did notice," she said, "But I noticed as well the cot-quilt was pink."

Elsie was taken aback; before she had time to think of a suitable explanation the bell rang and the opportunity was lost.

Anna's world was restored to its proper happy perspective once again. Babies *did* bring love and joy and tenderness, and they *were* heavenly. The important thing was to marry somebody as nice as Mr. Luke.

CHAPTER NINETEEN

NEW WORLDS IN SIGHT

Anna's and Elsie's days at the village school were drawing to an end. Shortly they would be involved in that awe-inspiring project known as 'sitting the scholarship.' Each year, two or three boys and girls approaching eleven years of age were selected by their head-teachers and allowed the privilege of trying to gain entrance to the boys' grammar school or the girls' high school at Oakdale. The successful ones were few and far between at Lowridge, Betty Butterfield having been the most recent one, except for Minnie who had to decline the offer. Anna's three brothers and one sister had in their time achieved this distinction but they had first attended school at Thickley with higher educational standards and more enlightened methods.

Anna was determined to become a teacher like her much admired brother. She was particularly eager to go to college for Philip had told such wonderful tales of his college days. The fun and gaiety of the communal life, the tricks played on the 'freshers,' the daring exploits of some young 'bloods' had caught her fancy; the important-sounding titles of their teachers—professors, dons and tutors—all seemed to belong to a most fascinating world that she was determined to enter.

Although Philip's college had been only some twenty-five miles away it seemed a great distance and an exciting adventure to the little country-bred girl who had never been so far from home, except for her trips to the seaside. Though it was such a thrilling prospect, she used to torture herself by imagining the agony it would be to leave her dear Greenfield, with its so intimately known fields, streams and hedgerows— and to leave her mother and all the family.

But that was in the far distant future; first get over the big hurdle into the high school.

Mr. Luke was very keen to get one or two of his most promising pupils through the exam, and concentrated steadily on their instruction in the term approaching it. Arithmetic and English were the qualifying subjects, and for several weeks the four 'chosen ones' did little else.

The prospect of secondary education was either held in awe or completely ignored by most of the parents, who had little idea of anything beyond their own meagre schooling in the village or similar schools of their childhood. Very few had any ambition for their children to go on with their education, but were anxious for them to get to work as soon as possible to add a welcome quota, however small, to the family budget.

"If I don't pass, father's going to pay for me to go," Anna confidently told Elsie. There were fee-paying places available for a few children each year, but even these were very limited.

"So's mine!" Elsie exulted.

"Oh, that'll be lovely!" Anna exclaimed. "Then we can always be best friends."

The daily train journey was an added delight to anticipate, and, like the girls who had gone to work in Oakdale, they cared little about the long walk to the station. They were already planning their future pleasures.

The novelty of wearing a school uniform appealed to them greatly. Compared with the odd assortment of garments that clothed the village children the uniformed pupils of the high school looked very smart indeed. Anna had seen a 'crocodile' of the latter once when shopping in Oakdale with her mother. She had regaled Elsie with a detailed description.

"Ooh! They did look nice, Elsie. They all had cream straw sailor hats on, with blue tunics, an' white blouses an' red ties, an' black stockings and black low shoes, Oh! I *hope* we go!"

It was an added incentive to work hard, and both girls strove hard to master the nouns, verbs, fractions and decimals so that they could do a test with speed and accuracy. They filled their compositions with flowery and fanciful phrases.

The first part of the examination was taken in their own school under the vigilance of the Master. The papers were then sent to the county education office and then came the awful suspense of waiting to hear who had to proceed to part two. The news came about a month later and, of the four candidates, Anna, Elsie and Harry were successful.

It was with some trepidation that they set out on the second lap, for this time the exam was held in a school in Oakdale. Arrayed in their best clothes, armed with new pens, pencils and rubbers and a goodly supply of sandwiches they departed, with the good wishes of all. They were rather tense and nervous, the girls' nods alternating between giggles and near tears, Harry trying a swagger that did not quite come off.

St. Hild's School, where they were to 'sit,' was, to their ideas, 'a great big place' seemingly swarming with pupils and teachers. Certainly there were enough to over-awe the young visitors from various rural schools who banded together in mutual shyness in the playground until summoned to their places for the fateful 'papers.'

Anna's nervousness soon left her as she found little to alarm her in the questions. Her pen glided smoothly and purposefully over the paper. The weeks of hard work had prepared her for something much more difficult. She had finished, checked and re-checked her answers before the decisive 'pens down' was uttered. Elsie and Harry seemed to have fared equally well, though Elsie was not very confident. However they all enjoyed the journey home.

With a vast sense of relief they got back to normal routine. The village school, they now saw, was small, dull and shabby, but strangely enough it seemed more likeable, safer and altogether more homelike after this, their first brief venture into a town school.

It was the next to last week of the term when the long, buff envelope bearing the county crest arrived at the school. Mr. Luke was over the moon with delight, for all three had passed the second stage, a feat previously unknown in the school's history. The wonderful news was announced at assembly and the three blushing victors, trembling with excitement and joy, had to go out for a clap.

Now all that remained was for them to attend an interview at their prospective secondary schools, and as this merely consisted of a little reading aloud and the answering of some common-sense questions, Mr. Luke had no doubts about their final success.

If St. Hild's had impressed them, the ancient grammar school and the very new girls' high school completely bowled them over!

All the way home they babbled about the wonders they had seen. The girls marvelled at the shiny, polished floors, the shiny new desks—one for each—lovely pictures, tiled cloakrooms with hot and cold taps, a gymnasium, a hall with a real stage and a separate dining room!

Harry got a word in here and there, about the oak panelled walls, the lofty hall with black oak beams, the gym with its rows of silver cups and the big, smooth playing field.

They just simply *must* have passed! The glimpse of so wonderful a world, peopled by such superior-looking girls and boys in their neat clothes, and such dignified teachers in their mysterious black gowns could not have been vouchsafed them just to mock them!

Summer holidays were approaching. The annual exams had been held and the last few days of glorious hot weather were spent in luxurious semi-idleness unknown in Mr. Black's day. Lessons were taken out of doors, the children sprawling, hot and perspiring, on the field behind the school, permission having been grudgingly given by its owner.

"We 'ad to work in *my* school days—none o' this new-fangled nonsense about *enjoyin'* lessons," he commented sourly. He was slightly appeased by Mr. Luke's gesture of allowing, albeit unofficially, three of the biggest boys to absent themselves to help with his haymaking. The shortage of able-bodied men on the farms was being felt most acutely.

Mr. Luke organized cricket matches between boys and girls; they sang out of doors, launched on the right note by the aid of a tuning fork; they read all the old favourite library books. Altogether it was quite blissful. Anna, Elsie and some more of the ones about to leave were almost tearful when they talked about their departure. Forgotten were all the 'old unhappy things, and battles long ago,' the poverty, shabbiness of their companions, equipment and surroundings. The known became increasing dear as the unknown drew nearer.

And so after goodbyes were said all around, their days at Lowridge Church of England School were over.

During the holidays both the girls and Harry were to receive the final, official confirmation that they had truly 'passed the scholarship' which would open up to them an exciting, new and different world of education.

But for the two girls there was—mingled with the happiness of the prospect—a fleeting nostalgic wish that they might still continue to be called to the little familiar school by the 'tin-tin-tin' which already seemed like faintly distant music to them.

~ ~ ~